Celebrating Our Diversity

Using Multicultural Literature to Promote Cultural Awareness

Grades K-2

by Marti Abbott and Betty Jane Polk

Richard P. Murphy, Series Consultant

FEARON TEACHER AIDS

Simon & Schuster Education Group

Marti Abbott received her Bachelor of Arts degree from Chico State University in California and her Master's degree from California State University, Sacramento. She traveled extensively in Europe and the Middle East, while teaching at the American Community School in Beirut. Participating in a joint U.S.-China conference on Education afforded her the opportunity to observe schools in China as well. Ms. Abbott, a mentor teacher, is now teaching kindergarten at Sierra Vista School in Vacaville, California.

Betty Jane Polk received her Bachelor of Arts degree from Chico State University in California and her Master's degree from California State University , Sacramento, where she and Ms. Abbott first developed their writing partnership. Ms. Polk has traveled throughout the United States and Central America. She is retired from the Davis School District in Davis, California, where she was the Director of the Parent Cooperative Preschool Program,

Richard P. Murphy is Coordinator of Global Education Programs for the Heartland Area Education Agency in Des Moines, Iowa. His publications, *A Guide to Teaching the Lao* and the *English/Lao Resource Book*, are used in schools around the world. His interest in cultures was sparked by his service in the Peace Corps in Thailand and he is the current secretary for the National Council of Returned Peace Corps Volunteers. Mr. Murphy has visited over twenty-five countries. In 1988, he was a Fulbright participant developing collaborative programs with China and in 1990 the Taiwan government sponsored his visit with Taiwan educators. He speaks Thai and Lao and is currently studying Chinese and Japanese.

Editorial Director: Virginia L. Murphy
Editor: Carol Williams
Copyeditor: Lisa Schwimmer
Illustration: Janet Skiles
Design: Diann Abbott
Cover Design and Illustration: Lucyna Green

ISBN 0-86653-989-1

Printed in the United States of America
1. 9 8 7 6 5 4 3

Acknowledgments

A special thanks to the following reviewers who have provided insight in their areas of expertise.

Dr. Barbara Cruz is a former teacher and consultant and is currently a global education instructor at the University of South Florida. Her roots are Cuban and her specialty areas are the Caribbean and Latin America. She lives in Tampa, Florida.

Maria Alicia Garcia-May is currently a classroom teacher with expertise on the Hispanic culture and the southwestern United States. She lives in San Benito, Texas.

Rulester Davis is a returned Peace Corps Volunteer serving in Africa. She is an Egyptologist and speaks Swahili. She is African-American and currently lives in Decatur, Georgia.

Sachiko Tamura is a Japanese teacher who has lived in the United States for six years. She is a developer of curriculum materials and consults with businesses concerning the Japanese culture. Sachiko lives in Des Moines, Iowa.

Sherif Sabry Wassef was born and raised in Cairo, Egypt. He currently lives in San Mateo, California.

Shunyi Cui has a Master's degree in English as a Second Language from the University of Northern Iowa. He is Mandarin Chinese and currently lives in Emporia, Kansas.

Wallace Goode is a former Dean of Allegheny College who also served in the Peace Corps in Africa and the Solomon Islands. An African-American, Wallace currently lives in Chicago, Illinois.

Wayne Johnson speaks fluent Thai and Lao and has lived extensively throughout Southeast Asia. He works for the Bureau of Refugee Programs in Des Moines, Iowa.

Yonsue Hong-Brady was born and raised in Korea and is currently living in Davis, California.

Karen Levin is a classroom teacher. She lives in Petaluma, California.

William H. Bean is a retired teacher and principal and consultant for the Iowa Department of Education. He is a highly respected Native American educator and currently lives in Des Moines, Iowa.

Contents

Introduction

Celebrating Our Diversity provides students with an exciting look into the diversity of our own country, as well as around the world, through multicultural literature. Multicultural literature helps students grow in an understanding of themselves and others. Books about children and their diverse cultures help develop children's identity and raise their level of self-esteem.

We need to teach children that there is more than one way to build a house, go to market, cook food, dress, and travel from place to place. Multicultural literature provides insights into the unique and valuable differences between cultures. Children learn through these valuable books and benefit greatly from the insights, experiences, and interests of others.

While our differences make us unique, our similarities bind us together. Multicultural literature helps children recognize and appreciate the many similarities we all share, such as the need for food, clothing, shelter, and love. And, most importantly, children learn that people everywhere share the same emotions. Cliff Roberts sums it up best in his book *Start with a Dot* when he writes,

> "The world is made of towns like these
> Filled with many families.
> Their faces are different,
> Their names are, too.
> But they laugh and cry
> The same as you!"

Literature has long been used as a vehicle for fostering cultural awareness, but often the presentation of the literature is both the beginning and the end. Teachers and students read multicultural books, but sometimes little consideration is given to the celebration of the cultural values, traditions, and beliefs inherent in these stories. It is our hope that this resource will widen your students' vision, deepen their understanding, and extend their experiences with diverse cultures.

Getting Started

Here is a brief overview of each of the components of this resource, with some hints and suggestions for their use.

Synopsis

This section gives you a quick look at what each story is all about. It also includes a reference as to whether the text in the book is provided in more than one language.

Background

Before reading each story, point out for the children where the story takes place. A small map identifying the location of the story is provided on the first page of each lesson. If possible, have a large world map available in your classroom for children to use as a reference. This section also provides information about the author and interesting cultural facts that relate to the story.

Deepen Your Understanding

This section provides four topics of discussion to use after sharing each story with your class. Information that is referenced in the stories, either by text or illustration, should be discussed with your students. The critical-thinking and discussion questions are intended to stimulate students to think a bit deeper and relate what they learn in the stories to their own lives. The questions are simply meant as a vehicle to get you started. Be sure to concentrate on the central message of each story as well. Keep in mind that these books are representations of the various cultures.

Extend Your Experience

Four activities are provided for each story to give your students a taste of a culture they may not have experienced before. Take advantage of community resources whenever possible. For example, when children are making a replica of a piece of folk art, try to locate the authentic item for display. Often, authentic items can be purchased at import stores, or pictures of the items can be located in your school or local library. Invite parents and cultural experts to share with your class to further extend the experience as well.

As a teacher, you need not be an expert in every culture featured in this book. You need simply have an open mind and an interest in introducing children to the diversity in this country and around the world.

DIVERSITY
In Common
EXPERIENCES

Bread Bread Bread

Written by Ann Morris and photographed by Ken Heyman
New York: Lothrop, Lee & Shepard, 1989

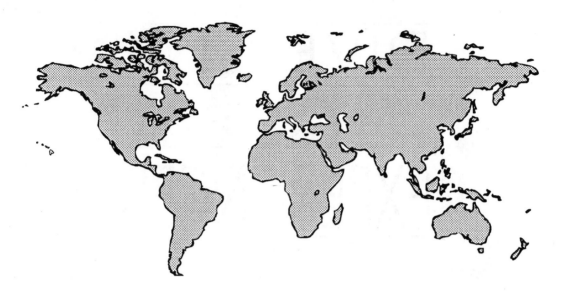

Synopsis

From Los Angeles to France to Hong Kong, people all over the world share a special fondness for bread. This photographic tour provides a wonderful opportunity to observe people everywhere enjoying the many different shapes, sizes, and textures of various breads.

Background

Bread (and also rice) are eaten in more places and in greater amounts than any other food. It can be made from wheat, rye, oat, or barley flour. It can be made with or without yeast (unleavened). It can take many different forms and names. Bread can be found in almost every country around the world.

Deepen Your Understanding

1. The main ingredient in bread is flour, although the type of flour from bread to bread may vary. Making bread can include measuring, kneading, rising, punching, shaping, and baking. Invite students to imagine they are bread bakers in several different countries. Ask children to consider what skills or knowledge their bread-baking jobs would require.

- Have you ever baked bread or seen someone bake bread?
- What kind of bread would you like to make? Why?
- What do you think is the most important ingredient in bread?
- How long do you think it would take to make bread? Why?
- What would you need to do to make a delicious loaf of bread?

2. The story reminds us that not only is bread enjoyed by people all over the world, but it is a food that is universally good for you. Bread provides carbohydrates which are necessary to give us energy. Bread provides minerals to keep our blood healthy and calcium for strong bones. Bread also provides fiber which keeps our digestive systems working properly. Invite students to recall the types of breads they have eaten in the past few days.

   - What kind of bread can you remember eating in the past few days?
   - What kind of bread have you eaten today?
   - What is your favorite kind of bread? Why?
   - Why do you think bread is good for you?
   - What other foods are good for you?

3. Encourage students to notice the various ways bread is transported or carried from place to place in the story. For example, in Ecuador, a woman carries unwrapped bread in a basket on her head. In Israel, a man carries his bread to market on a bicycle. Invite students to compare and contrast the different ways bread is packaged and brought to market in the different countries.

   - How do you think bread gets to your supermarket?
   - How is it packaged? How is bread packaged differently in the story?
   - How do you take bread home from the supermarket?
   - How much do you think a loaf of bread costs? Do you think the price is the same in all parts of the world? Why or why not?
   - Do some breads cost more than others? Why?
   - If you were going to sell bread, what kind would you sell? How would you get your bread to the market? How much would it cost?

4. Bread is not only eaten plain, but is also used to make many other delicious foods as well. French bread can be used to make sandwiches. Bread dough is sometimes turned into pizza by adding a few toppings. Several of the breads in Hong Kong have sweet fillings tucked inside them. Ask children to consider all the different foods that are made from bread.

   - What other foods are made from bread?
   - What do you like to put on a slice of bread?
   - What is your favorite kind of sandwich? Tell us how to make it.

Extend Your Experience

Making Chappatties

Unleavened bread is made without using any yeast. It is flatter and heavier than leavened bread. Read *Bread Bread Bread* again and invite children to notice which breads appear to be unleavened (Peruvian bread, chappatties, Sicilian bread, and tortillas). Ask students what types of unleavened bread they have eaten. Make chappatties with the class and enjoy them together.

Chappatties	
• 1 ½ cups (375 ml) whole wheat flour	Mix the flour and salt together. Gradually stir in the water until dough forms into a soft
• ½ tsp (2.5 ml) salt	ball. Knead the dough for 5-10 minutes on a
• ⅔ cup (180 ml) warm water	floured surface. Let the dough rise in a covered bowl for about 30 minutes. Then cut
• oil	the dough into six pieces. Roll each piece into
	an eight-inch circle. Place a small amount of
	oil in a frying pan, just enough to cover the
	bottom. Heat the pan until it begins to
	smoke. Cook the dough circles, one at a time,
	until they are brown and puffy on both sides.

Bread Is Bread

Using the information in the back of *Bread Bread Bread*, point to the bread pictures and identify the bread names (roll, loaf, baguette, pita, pizza, chappatties, pretzel, toast, tortillas, and challah). Ask students to share the names of other types of breads they know as well. Remind students of other kinds of breads they may be familiar with, such as biscuits, crackers, muffins, pancakes, and waffles. Also share some types of breads that may be new to students. For example,

croissants (crescent-shaped rolls made with delicate, buttery dough)

grissini (thin, crunchy, Italian bread sticks)

bagels (chewy, doughnut-shaped rolls)

crumpets (thin batter cooked on a hot griddle—similar to English muffins)

olykoeks (sweet dough fried in deep fat; olykoeks were brought to this country by the Dutch and are called "doughnuts" in the United States)

pumpernickel (dark, heavy, German rye bread)

Holiday Bread

In many countries, festivals or holidays provide an occasion for baking and eating special breads. For example, in *Bread, Bread Bread*, a Tel Aviv family celebrates the Sabbath by breaking bread together. Prayers are said over the special bread called "challah." Challah is a beautiful yellow braid of bread made without fruit or nuts.

It would not be Easter in Russia without kulich. Kulich is a tall, round-topped loaf of bread that looks like a mushroom. The Irish have a favorite bread called "barmbrack" that is served at Halloween. A special bread called "stollen" is served in Germany at Christmas. It is a sweet bread full of candied fruits and nuts.

Encourage children to share stories about special breads eaten in their homes during festivals or holidays. Invite children to bring in samples of these breads—or bring in the recipes. Have parent volunteers help the class bake and sample these special treats.

Bread Collage

- pictures of breads from magazines and newspapers
- glue
- scissors
- posterboard

Invite students to collect pictures of a variety of sizes, shapes, and types of breads from magazines and newspapers. After a sizeable collection has been gathered, encourage students to work in cooperative groups to sort and classify the bread pictures. Make a posterboard collage to represent each classification, such as round bread, crunchy bread, or "bread I would like to try."

Everybody Cooks Rice

Written by Norah Dooley and illustrated by Peter J. Thornton
Minneapolis: Carolrhoda, 1991

Synopsis

Carrie's stomach is growling, but before she and her family can eat dinner, Carrie must search the neighborhood for her brother Anthony. As she goes from house to house, she samples each family's dinner. Through her multicultural dinnertime adventure, Carrie realizes that everybody cooks rice, yet each dish is unique.

Background

Norah Dooley was inspired to write this story after hosting a neighborhood potluck dinner. Five of her guests arrived with a rice dish—each from a different country. In the story, the neighborhood families have roots in Barbados, Puerto Rico, Vietnam, India, China, Haiti, and Italy.

Deepen Your Understanding

1. Carrie and Anthony knew their neighbors and felt comfortable visiting their homes. They enjoyed listening to their neighbors' stories and playing with their neighbors' children and grandchildren. Encourage children to feel the sense of comradery and "family" Carrie and Anthony shared with their neighbors and to compare this experience to an experience they may have had recently.

- How well do you know your neighbors?
- Do you think they do things the same way that you do?
- Do you have some friends from your neighborhood that you like to play with? Who?
- Have you ever learned something new from a neighbor? What?

2. Each family that Anthony and Carrie visited was preparing one of their favorite dinners. Although each family was using rice in some way, the flavors varied greatly. Invite children to discuss which rice dish they would most enjoy tasting and then tell what their favorite dinner would be.

- Which rice dish would you like to taste?
- Which rice dish do you think would taste the best? Why?
- What is your favorite dinner?
- Do you think other people would enjoy your favorite dinner? Why or why not?
- What other foods, besides rice, can be cooked in many ways?

3. Each family in the story had dinner schedules and habits based on their lifestyle. In the Diaz home, Fendra and Tito were cooking dinner because their mom was working late. At the Tran home, everyone took turns cooking dinner because Mr. and Mrs. Tran both worked late. The Huas used chopsticks to eat their meal. Encourage children to share their own dinner schedules and habits.

- When do you usually eat dinner? Why?
- Do you help with dinner at your home? What's your job?
- What do you put on the table when you set the table for dinner?
- Who usually eats dinner with you?
- Is there anything you would change about dinnertime at home if you could? What? Why?

4. In the story, Mr. and Mrs. D are from Barbados. The Diaz family is from Puerto Rico. Dong Tran comes from Vietnam, and Rajit is from India. The Huas come from China and the Bleus are from Haiti. Carrie and Anthony have family roots in Italy. Encourage children to find out and discuss where they each come from. Help children locate the places on a world map, if possible.

- Can you find all the places the families in the story are from on a map?
- Do you know anybody that has visited any of these places?
- Which place would you most like to visit? Why?
- What country did your family come from?

Extend Your Experience

Let's Make Rice

- recipes and ingredients for rice dishes from recipes in *Everybody Cooks Rice*

Carrie had the opportunity to sample many delicious rice dishes as she went from neighbor to neighbor looking for Anthony. Each rice recipe is provided in the back of *Everybody Cooks Rice*. Invite students to collectively decide which recipe or recipes they would like to try. Make a list of the ingredients needed and ask for volunteers to bring the necessary items to school from home. Enjoy making the recipes together in class. If your students would like to try more than one recipe, invite parent volunteers to help. After children have tried several new rice dishes, make a graph showing each child's favorite. Encourage children to talk about rice dishes that are prepared in their homes.

Kitchen Craft

- measuring cup with standard and metric units
- wooden spoon
- ladle
- measuring spoons

Invite children to notice and name the tableware and cooking utensils used in the story (ladle, measuring spoons, tiffin carrier, wok, chopsticks, wooden spoon). Display the kitchen utensils listed and ask students to describe how each is used. Ask children whether or not everybody uses the same cooking utensils when they prepare meals. Point out that some measuring cups use standard units of measure and some use metrics.

Invite children to choose a small cooking utensil that is used to prepare meals in their home and bring it to school to share with the class. Encourage students to choose a utensil they think might be unique. Have students explain and demonstrate how the utensil is used.

Doesn't Everybody?

- construction paper
- lined paper
- crayons or markers
- stapler

According to the story, everybody cooks rice. Ask children what else they think everybody does, such as eat, sleep, or play. Make a classroom booklet showing the diversity in these similarities. For example, invite each student to contribute a page that illustrates or describes his or her family. Appreciate the variety of family structures that include grandparents, aunts, uncles, cousins, and stepparents. Show worldwide diversity by making a booklet called, "Everybody Needs a Place to Live." Do some research with the children to find out about different homes around the world. Invite students to draw pictures or write descriptions to make a page for each type of home.

All About Rice

- baggies
- rice (long grain, short grain, converted, instant, brown, and so on)

Rice is available in many different varieties. Each has a different look and nutritional value. Brown rice is the most nutritious, as the bran and protein have not been removed. Instant rice has been pre-cooked and dehydrated for faster preparation. Converted rice has been parboiled to enrich the grains with minerals from the bran. Long-grain rice remains separate when cooked, while short-grain rice is sticky. Provide a few grains of each kind of rice in a baggie for children to pass around and observe. Discuss the differences and similarities.

Hats Hats Hats

Written by Ann Morris and photographed by Ken Heyman
New York: Lothrop, Lee & Shepard, 1989

Synopsis

This book takes a photographic look at hats around the world. It also provides a look at the faces of the people who wear the hats, the places in which they live, and how they use the hats to help them work and play.

Background

Hats can be worn to provide protection from the sun, show respect, or just add a decorative touch. Whatever the reason, hats are worn by people all around the world and come in all sizes, shapes, and colors.

Deepen Your Understanding

1. The story points out that not only are there many types of hats, but there are many reasons for wearing them. A construction worker in the United States wears a "hard hat" to protect him or her from falling objects. An Egyptian man might wear a kaffiyeh to protect himself from the hot desert sun. And, in Nigeria, a special chicken feather hat might be worn for celebration. Invite students to think of other reasons for wearing hats.

   - When was the last time you wore a hat? Why were you wearing it?
   - Which of the hats in the story would you like to wear? Why?

- What other reasons can you think of for wearing a hat?
- Can you tell something about a person by the type of hat he or she is wearing? What?

2. The photographs in the story show a marvelous collection of hats worn by all types of people in many lands. Invite students to name other items they might collect.

- Why do you think people around the world wear hats?
- What other types of things do you think people around the world might wear?
- What are some other things that people around the world have in common?
- If you could collect anything from around the world, what would you collect? If you were to write a book about it, like *Hats Hats Hats*, what would you call your book? What kinds of photographs would you put in your book?

3. The story shows only a few of the many hats worn by people around the world. Invite children to name and describe other hats they may have seen or heard about. Encourage students to invent some new hats as well.

- Do you know the names of some other hats that are not pictured in the story? What?
- If you were asked to invent a hat, what would it look like? What would you use your hat for?
- What is the most unusual hat you have ever seen?
- Which type of hat do you think is worn the most? Why?
- Do you have any hats? What kind?

4. Hats can be made from a variety of fabrics and materials. Some hats are made from leather, some from wool, and some from straw. Other hats are made from paper. Some are made from plastic. Show students the photographs in the story once again and invite them to guess what each hat is made from.

- Why do you think hats are made from so many different kinds of materials?
- What kind of fabric or material would you use if you were going to make a hat to keep you warm?
- What kind of hat fabric do you think will last the longest? Why?

Extend Your Experience

Fiesta Pom-Pom Hats

- 9" (22.9 cm) paper plates
- paper bowls
- yarn (assorted colors)
- scissors
- hole punch
- rulers
- crayons or markers

Hats from other lands are fascinating to look at and fun to make and wear. Give each student a paper plate. Cut out the center of each paper plate so that the rim fits the child's head. Punch 8 to 10 holes, evenly spaced, around the rim of each plate. Have children wrap yarn loosely around a ruler twelve times and then slip the yarn off the ruler, making sure the loops of yarn remain intact. Slip an 8" (20.4 cm) piece of yarn through the yarn loops and tie securely. Cut the loops at the opposite end. Trim and fluff to make a neat pom-pom. Invite students to each make 8 pom-poms, then tie the pom-poms to the holes in the rims of their hats. Then show children how to glue paper bowls over the holes in the tops of the hats. Encourage children to add colorful decorations to their hats using crayons or markers and then enjoy wearing them. For a whole collection of fun and easy hats to make and wear, use the teacher resource *Hats, Hats, and More Hats* by Jean Stangl (see the bibliography on page 207).

Hat Collage

- pictures of hats from magazines and newspapers
- glue
- scissors
- posterboard

Invite students to collect pictures of a variety of sizes, shapes, and types of hats from magazines and newspapers. After a sizeable collection has been gathered, divide the class into cooperative groups and encourage children to sort and classify the hat pictures. Make a class posterboard collage to represent each classification, such as hats for play, work, or hats from other countries.

Hats International

- world map
- push pins
- paper
- crayons or markers

A special day in January is set aside each year to observe "National Hat Day." Set aside a special "International Hat Day" in your classroom. Invite children to wear a hat or head covering to school that is characteristic of another culture. Give each child an opportunity to talk about where his or her hat is from and any other interesting information, such as what the hat is made of or when it is usually worn. Invite each student to mark the origin of his or her hat on the world map.

Crown of Honor

- 12" x 18" (30.5 cm x 45.9 cm) yellow construction paper
- glitter
- star stickers
- scissors
- stapler

Though hats are worn for many practical reasons, such as for shade from the sun or for safety, some are worn to show honor to the wearer and to make him or her feel special. Design a special classroom crown for children to wear on special occasions. For example, make a special crown for children to wear on their birthdays. Or, invite each student to make a crown to wear on a specially designated "Crown Day."

Have each student cut a 12" x 18" (30.5 cm x 45.9 cm) sheet of construction paper in half lengthwise. Staple the short edges together to make one long strip that is 6" (15.3 cm) wide. Invite students to cut an interesting design along one long edge and then add sparkly stars and glitter. Wrap the crown around each child's head and carefully staple the edges together for a perfect fit. On "Crown Day," encourage children to share one characteristic about themselves that makes them unique and special. Choose a positive quality you have noticed in each student and pay each child a special and personal compliment.

Loving

Written by Ann Morris and photographed by Ken Heyman
New York: Lothrop, Lee & Shepard, 1990

Synopsis

People around the world may wear different clothing, eat different foods, and play different games, but they show their love for each other in similar ways. The beautiful photographs in this book depict people from around the world helping, talking, listening, and sharing with one another.

Background

This multicultural glimpse into basic human needs around the world helps children realize that our similarities as human beings are much more important than our differences. From Guatemala to Israel to Hong Kong, we all need to feel loved.

Deepen Your Understanding

1. One way the book suggests that we show love is by listening to what others have to say. For example, the father in Texas listens as his son tells him what he wants to be when he grows up. Encourage children to recall times their friends or family members have shown love to them by being good listeners.

   - Who listens to you when you have something to share?
   - Who do you most enjoy listening to?
   - How do you feel when no one will listen to you?

- Are you a careful listener when others are telling you what is important to them? Who do you listen to?

2. Moms and dads all around the world take care of their children by giving them food, keeping them clean and tidy, and making sure they are dressed and cozy. Invite children to think of ways their families care for them.

- How does your family take care of you?
- What is the most important thing your family does for you?
- How do you help care for other members of your family?
- What are some things you need from your family that you think children all over the world need from their families?

3. People who love you often spend time teaching you things that you need to know. The Israeli father in the story is teaching his son how to read, for example. Encourage children to talk about what they learn from their families.

- Has anyone in your family ever taught you how to do something? What?
- What would you like someone to teach you?
- Which of the new things the children are learning in the story would you like to learn? Why?
- Have you ever taught someone in your family how to do something? What?

4. Family members often help you when you are feeling sad by giving hugs, talking to you, or doing things to make you laugh. Invite children to realize that children all over the world, regardless of the way they look or dress, laugh and cry just like they do.

- Who makes you laugh?
- What makes you feel sad?
- Who makes you feel better when you are feeling sad?
- Besides being happy and sad, what other emotions do you feel? Do you think children who live in other places around the world have these feelings, too? Why or why not?

Extend Your Experience

Love Bouquets

- small juice cans
- red, white, and pink construction paper
- popsicle sticks
- glue
- scissors
- pencils, crayons, and markers
- clay dough
- glitter, yarn, stickers (optional)

Invite children to make bouquets of hearts for friends or family members as a way of saying "thank you" for the love they give. Cut

strips of construction paper the same width as a small juice can is tall and long enough to wrap all the way around the can. Have students glue the strips around juice cans to cover them completely. Encourage the children to decorate their cans using the materials listed.

Invite children to cut pairs of different-sized hearts from colored construction paper. Encourage students to write "I love you because . . ." on one of their pairs of hearts. Have students glue these two hearts back to back on either side of the end of a popsicle stick. Then have students write or dictate other reasons why they are thankful to those who show them love on other pairs of hearts. For example, children may write " . . . you tuck me in my bed at night," " . . . you make my favorite dinner," or " . . . you sing to me when I'm sad." Have students glue these hearts back to back as well on a popsicle stick. Students can add stickers, yarn designs, or glitter to their heart messages, if they wish.

Fill the covered juice cans with enough clay dough so that when the popsicle sticks are inserted, the hearts stick up above the rims of the cans at varying heights. Encourage the children to deliver their love bouquets as a way of saying "I love you."

Love in Any Language

Though the terms for love vary around the world, the concept is universal and understood by people of all nationalities. Encourage children to learn to say "I love you" in several different languages. To say "I love you" in sign language, extend the pointer finger, little finger, and thumb of one hand with the palm facing outward. Keep the two middle fingers curled down.

"I love you" in French is pronounced "zhuh▪TEM"
"I love you" in Korean is pronounced "sah▪LAWNG▪hay▪yo"
"I love you" in Spanish is pronounced "tay AH▪moh"
"I love you" in Vietnamese is pronounced "toy▪tooung▪em"

Love in Action

- drawing paper
- crayons or markers

Children play and care for their pets in loving ways as shown in the story. Children often have very strong feelings for their pets, favorite dolls, or stuffed animals. Children can easily relate to the role of caretaker in these situations. Invite children to draw a picture of themselves caring for a pet, favorite doll, or stuffed animal. Encourage students to write or dictate along the bottom of the picture a sentence that describes how they take care of something they love. Display the pictures on a bulletin board entitled "Love in Action."

Teach Me How

In the story, parents teach their children new skills, such as how to read, count, ride a pony, and build an airplane. Older children sometimes help younger children as a way of showing their love as well. Invite children to think of a special skill they have that they could teach a classmate as a way of showing friendship. For example, a student could teach a classmate how to snap his or her fingers, make a cup from paper, sing a song, or play a song on an instrument. If some of your students have strong roots in their cultural heritage, the skills they teach their classmates can extend children's understanding of the world around them.

DIVERSITY In AMERICA

Cornrows

Written by Camille Yarbrough and illustrated by Carole Byard
New York: Coward-McCann Inc., 1979

Synopsis

Sister and her little brother, MeToo, learn the richness of their African-American heritage as Mama and Great-Grammaw tell some "se-ri-ous, dy-no-mite" stories while weaving the children's hair into striking cornrow patterns. Every design has a name that represents a powerful African-American tradition.

Background

Many years ago, slave traders captured many Black Africans and shipped them to America as slaves. These Black Africans were stripped of their cultural roots and separated from their families, friends, and independent life. Slavery was abolished in the United States in 1865. *Cornrows* is a story about a part of Black African heritage.

Deepen Your Understanding

1. Sister and her little brother, MeToo, loved to hear their Mama and Great-Grammaw tell stories. Storytelling is a common characteristic of many cultures. The storytelling tradition is a way of passing along one's cultural heritage from generation to generation.

- Why do you think Sister and MeToo enjoyed listening to the stories so much?
- Have you ever heard someone in your family tell a real-life story about something that happened long ago?
- Do you have any interesting real-life stories that you like to tell?
- What kinds of stories do you like to listen to? Why?

2. Great-Grammaw told the story of the spirit that lives inside you. She told how Africans were packed on slave ships and brought across the sea. These Africans endured many hard times, but their determined spirits did not die. Help children understand the hardships African-Americans have faced over the years.

- How do you think the Africans felt when they were taken away from their homes and forced to work as slaves?
- Have you ever felt discouraged, sad, or that you were treated unfairly?
- What do you think it means that "their spirits did not die"?
- Have you ever felt like giving up? What did you do?

3. Cornrowed hair is one symbol of an African tradition from the Yoruba, who live in southwestern Nigeria and parts of Benin and Togo. The types of cornrow patterns and the number of braids tell something special about the person who is wearing them. Invite children to discuss other hairstyles they have seen or worn.

- Would you like to have your hair braided in cornrows?
- What is your favorite way to wear your hair?
- What other types of hairstyles have you seen?

4. In Africa, the symbols of carved sculptures and other art forms, such as dance and music, represent the spirit that lives within the people. The symbols live forever to represent courage, honor, wisdom, love, and strength. If possible, display some authentic African art forms, or plan a trip to a nearby museum. Or, review the pictures in the story that illustrate African symbols.

- Why are these African symbols so important?
- What do you think these symbols mean?
- What symbol would you make to represent the spirit that is inside you?

Extend Your Experience

MeToo!

MeToo always wanted to do exactly what his sister did. Ask children if they have ever tried to copy someone they admire. Point out the accomplishments of several of the people mentioned in the story.

Harriet Tubman was known as the "conductor" of the Underground Railroad that helped free slaves.

On December 1, 1955, Rosa Parks was taken to jail for refusing to give up her seat on a bus to a white man, as required by law.

Katherine Dunham was made famous for her interpretive African dance tours all over the world.

Marcus Garvey's original home was in Africa. He preached that Africans should go back to Africa to avoid the mistreatment they were receiving in America.

George Washington Carver was a truly great scientist. From his laboratory flowed many new discoveries and products, such as better ways to grow foods and new products made from peanuts, like soap, ink, and powder.

Mary McLeod Bethune became a White House Advisor to President Franklin D. Roosevelt. She also helped build the Bethune-Cookman College.

Just as MeToo wanted a model to follow, encourage children to view these role models as inspirations for their own lives. Invite children to tell who they admire most. Encourage children to name contemporary African-American leaders and role models as well, such as Magic Johnson, Maya Angelou, Jesse Jackson, or Oprah Winfrey.

Poetry Party

- collection of poetry by Langston Hughes, such as *Don't You Turn Back* or *The Dream Keeper*

Sister decided to name her hairstyle after Langston Hughes, an honored author in America. He wrote many poems about the pleasures, joys, and sorrows of life. Introduce students to Langston Hughes by giving a brief background and reading some of his poetry aloud. Memorize one of Langston Hughes' poems together as a class. "April Rain Song," found in both poetry collections named here, is a fun and easy poem for students to learn. Try adding hand motions that complement the poetic verse.

Cornrows

- yarn (or strips of cloth)
- masking tape

Cornrow braids were so named because they look like rows of corn in cornfields. The hairstyle is also called "suku" by the Yoruba, which actually means "basket." Children might enjoy the experience of learning how to braid if they have never done so. Tie three strands of yarn together at one end with a knot. (Younger children might find it easier to braid wider strips of cloth.) Tape the knotted end to the edge of each child's desk. Show children how to braid the three strands together and then knot the end when they are finished. Invite children to predict how long it might take to actually braid an entire cornrow hairstyle. Encourage children to appreciate the artistic work and talent of Great-Grammaw.

Rhythm and Rhyme

- empty oatmeal containers, boxes, cartons, and so on

The drum is a very important instrument in Africa, and there are many different kinds. For example, the "gangan" is a drum used by the Yoruba tribe. This drum is made from a hollow log with an animal hide stretched over the top. Invite students to create drums from available resources. An upside-down trash can, an empty oatmeal container, a box, or an empty ice-cream carton are all good materials to use. Encourage children to beat a steady rhythm on their drums as you reread the poetic sections of the story—"You can name it for a river, you can name it for a flower, for the year, for the month, for the day or for the hour. . . ," and so on.

Follow the Drinking Gourd

Written and illustrated by Jeanette Winter
New York: Alfred A. Knopf, 1988

Synopsis

At night, when the work was done, Peg Leg Joe taught American slaves a song that secretly told the way to freedom. Under a starry sky, many slaves began the journey, guided by the song lyrics, that eventually led them to freedom in Canada and the northern United States.

Background

The Underground Railroad was neither a railroad nor was it located underground. It was a network of people who helped slaves escape slavery by fleeing the South. Men and women risked their lives to "conduct" runaway slaves to different hiding places in homes, sometimes called "stations," on their way north. Stations were often identified by white chimneys with a black ring painted around the top. People like Peg Leg Joe left "tracks." Conductors, stations, and tracks combined to form a hidden (underground) path (tracks) of homes (stations) where brave men and women (conductors) led runaway slaves to freedom.

Deepen Your Understanding

1. Slaves had to hide from slave catchers and bounty hunters who made a business of returning runaway slaves to their owners. Many escaping slaves were assisted along the way in "safe houses" or "stations." These houses were the homes of people who believed slavery was wrong. They were willing to have these strangers stay in their homes or barns, even though there was great risk involved.

   - What is slavery?
   - Why do you think slaves ran away?
   - Why do you think people allowed the runaway slaves to stay in their homes when it could cause them trouble?
   - What would the slaves have done if no one would have allowed them in their homes?

2. Discuss slavery with your students.

   - Why do you think people wanted to have slaves?
   - Do you think it is right for people to own slaves? Why or why not?
   - How do you think the people who were sold as slaves felt?

3. Though escaping slaves faced many dangers, they often also encountered kind deeds. In the story, a young boy brought some bacon and corn bread to share with the travelers. Strangers would welcome the travelers into their homes for a safe night's rest.

   - Would you have wanted to do a kind deed for the slaves? Why or why not?
   - What could you have done to help the slaves?
   - When was the last time you did a kind deed? What did you do?
   - Has anyone ever done something special for you?
   - How did it make you feel?

4. The only safe way for Peg Leg Joe to convey his message of freedom was to disguise the map route in the words of a song. Discuss why secrecy was so important and encourage children to think about what might have happened if the masters had known what Peg Leg Joe was doing.

   - What are some ways people usually figure out where they are going?
   - Have you ever used a map?
   - Why do you think Peg Leg Joe used the words of a song instead of giving the slaves a map?
   - What do you think would have happened if the masters had found out what Peg Leg Joe was doing?

Extend Your Experience

Making a Freedom Train

- construction paper
- scissors
- glue
- crayons or markers

February 1 is National Freedom Day. This day is set aside to commemorate the issue by President Abraham Lincoln of the proclamation abolishing slavery in 1863. Ask children what freedom means to them. Challenge students to think of a definition for the word "freedom."

Cut a simple train engine from black construction paper and display it on a bulletin board entitled "Freedom Train." Give each student a rectangular piece of construction paper to make a train car. Invite children to write or dictate a sentence or draw a picture to describe what freedom means to them. For example, "Freedom means being able to ride my bike around the neighborhood," or "Freedom means having what I want for lunch." Display the train cars behind the engine on the bulletin board to form one long freedom train.

Follow the Drinking Gourd

- song in back of *Follow the Drinking Gourd*

Teach your students the song Peg Leg Joe taught the slaves. If possible, add some musical accompaniment. Or, teach your students the lyrics as a poem. Divide the class into four groups and invite each group to learn a verse. Memorizing the words to the song will give students the feeling of how the slaves passed along the message of freedom.

Reading the Stars

- dark blue or black construction paper
- star stickers
- compass

In the story, the slaves were taught a song that led them to freedom by following the stars. The stars were their maps. The Drinking Gourd is the Big Dipper, which points to the North Star. If the slaves followed the Drinking Gourd, they would be headed north, which was the direction of their destination—Canada.

Give each child a sheet of construction paper and some star stickers. Help the children make replicas of the Big Dipper constellation. Use a compass to find which way is north in the classroom. Display the Drinking Gourds on a bulletin board pointing north.

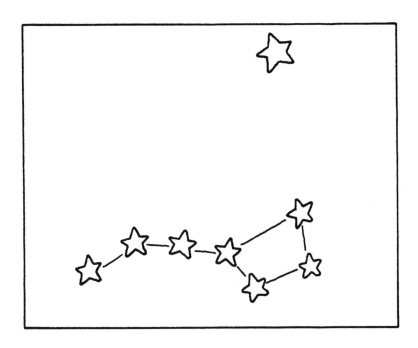

Remind students that the escaping slaves used the stars as a compass to point them in the right direction. Encourage children to look for the Big Dipper in the night sky.

Growing Cotton

- *Cotton* by Millicent E. Selsam
- fabric swatches
- posterboard

Cotton was an important crop in the South as depicted in the story. Before machinery was invented, the job of picking cotton was done by hand. Show children the pictures in Millicent E. Selsam's *Cotton* (see the bibliography on page 207) and describe how cotton grows. The plant has white blossoms that turn red, wither, and fall off the plant. The part of the flower that remains turns into a "boll." In about four months, the boll begins to split open. The cotton is then ready to be picked. Cotton is one of the world's most important textiles. It is a part of our daily lives, from the time we use a soft cotton towel in the morning until we go to bed on cotton sheets at night. Invite students to brainstorm a list of things they use everyday that are made from cotton, such as clothing, handkerchiefs, sheets, curtains, and so on.

Mount a variety of fabric swatches on posterboard. Invite students to feel each swatch and try to identify the ones that are cotton. Set aside a "Cotton Day" and encourage students to wear clothes that are made from cotton. There are local and national associations of weavers and spinners. Invite such an expert to your class. Or, identify a southern agricultural school and write and ask for samples of raw cotton for each student.

Just Plain Fancy

Written and illustrated by Patricia Polacco
New York: Bantam Books, 1990

Synopsis

As Naomi goes about her chores of caring for the chickens, she longs to have something fancy to contrast with her plain life in the Amish community. That very day, Naomi and her sister, Ruth, discover an extraordinary egg in the hen house. When this special egg hatches into a beautiful peacock, Naomi fears her "fancy" find will be shunned by her family.

Background

The largest concentration of Amish live in the beautiful rural areas of southeastern Pennsylvania. The Amish practice customs and beliefs that have been passed down through many generations that preserve a religious and plain, less complicated lifestyle. Patricia Polacco visited the Amish as she prepared to write this story.

Deepen Your Understanding

1. Amish families live without electricity or plumbing. Cooking is done by wood- or coal-burning stoves. Water must be brought in from outside for cooking, drinking, and bathing. Invite children to look closely at the illustrations in the story and notice the daily routines that seem different (riding in a buggy, washing clothes by hand, and so on).

- What are some things that you do differently than are done in the story (washing dishes, washing clothes, cooking, and so on)?
- What things do you use every day that are run by electricity?
- How would your life be different if you lived in an Amish community?

2. Children all over the world have dreams and wishes about how their lives might be different. Naomi was no exception. Naomi's wish was that she could have something very out-of-the-ordinary. She wanted something "fancy." Invite children to compare Naomi's feelings about wishing for something she did not have with their own desires and dreams.

- If you could change something about your life, what would it be?
- If you had one wish, what would it be?
- Have you ever gotten something you really wanted and then, like Naomi, wondered whether you should really have it?
- Do you think Naomi has other wishes? What?

3. Amish women and young girls often wear plain dresses with long sleeves and a full skirt. The dresses are solid, neutral colors, such as blue or brown. Dresses are rarely bright colors, such as red, yellow, pink or patterned. Under their neat caps, young girls wear their hair parted in the middle and braided. Men and boys often wear trousers with suspenders. Colored shirts are worn, but stripes and prints are not. The men wear various styles of brimmed hats.

- Why do you think the Amish dress as they do?
- Do you ever compare what you are wearing with what other people are wearing?
- Do you think the Amish compare their clothing? Why or why not?
- Have you ever worn a uniform or dressed to look exactly like everyone else? When?

4. Naomi was given a new white organdy cap because Martha said she had earned it. Naomi had given good and faithful care to her flock of chickens and she had raised one of the finest peacocks ever seen. Encourage children to recall some of their own accomplishments for which they have been recognized or rewarded.

- How do you think Naomi felt when Martha gave her the new white cap to wear? Do you think Naomi deserved the new cap? Why or why not?
- Have you ever been rewarded for something you did especially well? What? How did you feel?
- Naomi felt very proud. Have you ever felt proud? What did you do to make you feel that way?
- Naomi said she had learned many things that day. What do you think she learned?

Extend Your Experience

Making Shoo-Fly Pie

The Amish are famous for their wonderful pies and cakes. Most meals end with either a fruit pie or the well-known shoo-fly pie. Make this traditional Amish dish to enjoy with your students.

Shoo-Fly Pie	
• ½ cup (125 ml) dark molasses	Dissolve the baking soda in the boiling water. Add the molasses and eggs.
• ½ cup (125 ml) boiling water	Stir well and let cool. Pour this filling
• ½ tsp (5 ml) baking soda	into the unbaked pie shell. Combine
• 2 eggs	flour, brown sugar, and spices. Cut in
• 2 cups (500 ml) flour	the shortening to form a crumb
• ½ cup (125 ml) brown sugar	mixture. Sprinkle the crumb topping
• ¼ tsp (1.25 ml) mixed spices (cinnamon, ginger, nutmeg, salt, cloves)	over the syrup mixture. Bake at 350°F (180°C) for about 65 minutes.
• ¼ cup (60 ml) shortening	
• 9" (22.9 cm) unbaked pie shell	

Schnitzin

- apples
- peelers
- table knives
- cooking utensils

Working together is an important part of the Amish way of life. In *Just Plain Fancy*, the members of the community got together for a "working bee" or "frolic." On that special day, they all worked together to add a stable to the Vleckes' barn. Work-centered get-togethers are common. Amish children enjoy getting together for an apple "schnitzin," which is an apple peeling and cutting party. Invite each of your students to bring an apple from home. Decide as a group what you will make with the apples (applesauce, apple pie, baked apples, and so on). Invite children to experience the team-work attitude of the Amish by peeling, cutting, and making an apple treat together.

Make It Yourself

- baby-food jars with lids
- heavy cream
- bread
- plastic knives

The Amish make many of the things they need themselves and do not rely on machines run by electricity to do the work for them. Give your students an opportunity to make something for themselves that they would ordinarily find already made and packaged at the supermarket—butter.

Give each student a small baby-food jar filled with heavy cream, about 1" (2.5 cm) deep. Place the lid on each jar and invite children to shake the jars rapidly. In about 3 to 5 minutes, children should see a small ball of butter forming. Help the children remove the butter from their jars, spread it on bread, and enjoy their homemade treat. (You might also wish to make homemade bread using your favorite recipe!)

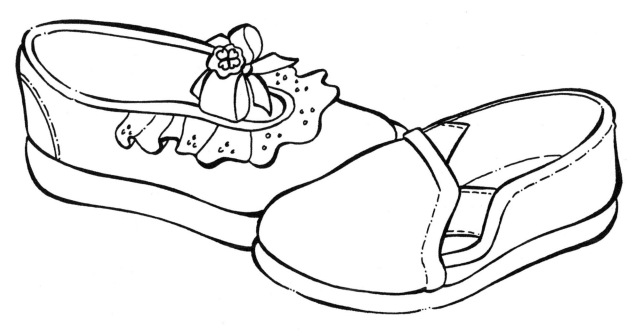

Plain or Fancy

- pairs of items (plain and fancy)

Help students understand that the Amish choose a plain lifestyle and that "plain" is a satisfactory way of life. Then present the children with a collection of pairs of items that come in both plain and fancy versions. For example, gather a yellow pencil, a white sheet of paper, a plain tennis shoe, and a baseball cap with no words or decorations on it. Then present a pencil with bright colors or sparkles; a colored or patterned piece of paper, such as gift wrap or stationery; a fancy dress shoe; and a decorative hat. Ask children why you have the items divided into the two groups. Discuss the difference between "plain" and "fancy." Point out that plain items are not inferior, just less fancy. Plain items often serve a more practical purpose. Invite students to add to the collection by bringing pairs of items from home that are plain and fancy (gloves, pillows, hair bands, cups, and so on).

The Flute Player: An Apache Folktale

Retold and illustrated by Michael Lacapa
Flagstaff, Arizona: Northland Publishing, 1990

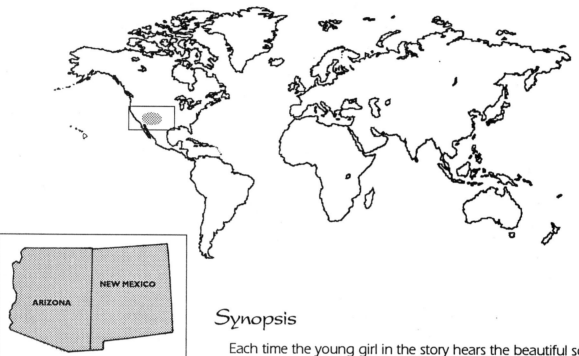

Synopsis

Each time the young girl in the story hears the beautiful sound of the boy's flute, she places a leaf in the river that runs through the canyon. As the leaf floats past the young flute player, he lifts it from the water and knows that his music was heard by the one he admires. One day, the flute player does not receive a leaf and soon learns that his beloved has died. The memory of the flute player's melody lives on in the beautiful sound of the wind blowing through the trees.

Background

The Apache today live in much of New Mexico and Arizona. Michael Lacapa has worked with the Apache developing educational materials. He is dedicated to preserving this story and others he has learned from the elders of the tribes.

Deepen Your Understanding

1. Ceremonies, mysteries, and medicine men were all part of early Native American life. Every tribe had medicine men and, in some cases, medicine women. In the story, the medicine man said special prayers and gave the young girl special medicine in hopes of healing her. Invite students to compare the medicine man in the story with doctors in their communities.

- When the young girl became ill, her family did everything they could to help heal her. What would your family do to help if you became ill?
- Do you have medicine men or women in your community? Who helps make you well?
- In the story, the young girl was so sad that she became ill. Do you think sadness can make you ill? Why or why not?
- Have you ever felt as sad as the young girl did? Have you ever had a good friend move away? How did you feel?
- If sadness can make you ill, do you think being happy can make you feel better? Why or why not?

2. Young Native American men were often taken by their uncles on hunting trips to teach them how to provide for a family in later life. They would first hunt small game, such as rabbits and birds. Later they would learn to hunt buffalo and deer. Encourage students to think about what they need to learn to be prepared for life as an adult.

- Why do you think the young boy needed to learn to hunt?
- Would you have liked to go on the hunting trip with the boy and his uncle? Why or why not?
- Do you need to learn to hunt?
- What do you need to learn to be prepared for life when you are older?

3. Corn, which is a very important food in this country, was first discovered by the Native Americans. The young girl in the story spent her days working in the cornfields. The tribes in the south-western United States valued their corn crops very highly and made sure there was always plenty of water to grow the corn.

- What does a corn plant look like?
- What do you think farmers who grow corn do to care for their crops?
- Would you like to work in a cornfield? Why or why not?
- What kind of crop would you like to grow? Why?
- Do you like to eat corn? Can you think of some things you eat that are made from corn?

4. The folktale ends by describing how people still go to the canyon to sit and listen to the echoes and watch leaves fall into the river. As the listeners hear the wind blowing, they are reminded of how much the young girl admired the flute player's sweet melody.

- What other sounds might the characters in the story have been able to hear?
- What sounds do you hear where you live?
- Are any of the sounds the same? Which ones are different?
- Have you ever heard a sound that reminded you of something else? What was the sound? What did the sound remind you of?
- Do you ever think the wind sounds like a flute? What does the sound of wind remind you of?

Extend Your Experience

Hoop Dance

- hula hoops
- recorders (optional)

The young couple in the story met at a hoop dance. A hoop dance can be done with one hoop or as many as 30. The dancers weave themselves in and out of the hoops as they dance. The hoops can also be intertwined to resemble flowers, insects, birds, or animals.

Invite students to work in small cooperative groups and choreograph a hoop dance. Encourage groups to perform their dances for the class. Students may want to add some "flute" music, using recorders, to enhance their steps.

Special Delivery

- paper
- pencils
- containers to use as drums
- small stones or pebbles

Invite students to brainstorm ways they usually send or receive messages from friends and family members (notes, letters, telephone, in person). The method of delivering a message in the story was a leaf traveling down a flowing river. Early southwest Native Americans sent messages to each other in many ways, such as using drums, smoke, picture writing, and clumping of stones. Encourage students to send messages using their own unique methods.

Have students work in pairs or small groups to devise an understandable code. For example, students might assign words or phrases to a particular pattern or rhythm of drum beats. Or, students could design simple picture symbols to represent words or ideas. Once a system is agreed upon by all group members, encourage students to practice sending and deciphering the special messages. Encourage students to also explain and demonstrate their code system to the rest of the class.

Flute Players

- "American Indian Flute Music" by High Eagle (Panoramic Sound)

In the Apache tribe, flute playing is often associated with courtship. If a girl mentions she likes a young man's flute music, then she also means that she likes him. She will then listen to no other flute player's music. The flute players often make up their own music. Give the children an opportunity to listen to some Native American flute music. Play some selections from "American Indian Flute Music" by High Eagle (distributed by Panoramic Sound, P.O. Box 58182, Houston, Texas 77258). Another good source of Native American music is Canyon Records (4143 North 16th Street, Phoenix, Arizona 85016). Or, check your local library. Invite students to imagine they are playing a flute while listening to the soothing sounds.

Making Corn Muffins

Corn was a valuable crop for the early Native Americans. Once the Apaches became farmers, they were able to settle in one area and no longer needed to move from place to place in search of food. The early Native Americans used corn in many ways. Some tribes would sweeten popcorn with maple sugar, inventing the first version of caramel corn. Make corn muffins with your class as a reminder of one of the wonderful ways to use the grain that was introduced to us by the natives of this land.

Corn Muffins	
• 1 ½ cups (325 ml) corn-meal	Mix all the ingredients and beat vigorously for about 30 seconds. Fill
• ½ cup (125 ml) flour	greased muffin tins about ¾ full and
• ¼ cup (60 ml) shortening	bake at 450°F (250°C) for 20
• 1 ½ cups (325 ml) butter-milk	minutes. This recipe makes about 14 full-size muffins or 30 mini-muffins.
• 2 tsp (10 ml) baking powder	
• 1 tsp (5 ml) salt	
• ½ tsp (2.5 ml) baking soda	
• 1 ½ tsp (7.5 ml) sugar	
• 2 eggs	

Appalachia: The Voices of Sleeping Birds

Written by Cynthia Rylant and illustrated by Barry Moser
New York: Harcourt Brace Jovanovich, 1991

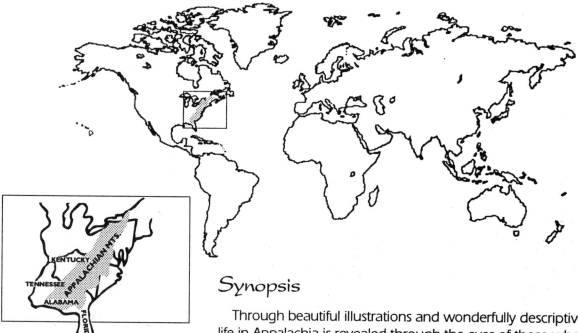

Synopsis

Through beautiful illustrations and wonderfully descriptive words, life in Appalachia is revealed through the eyes of those who have experienced it. On a typical day, people living in this remote mountainous region might enjoy a helping of fried chicken, linger in the yard after church to talk with friends and neighbors, and enjoy the sweet aroma of honeysuckle while traveling down a dirt road in the heart of summer.

Background

The Appalachian Mountains stretch from Quebec, Canada to central Alabama. This story takes place in the more remote part of this region in Tennessee and West Virginia. Cynthia Rylant and Barry Moser both grew up in Appalachia and draw upon their family backgrounds to create this quiet and picturesque story.

Deepen Your Understanding

1. Cynthia Rylant's story of Appalachia traces people's lives through each season of the year. In the spring, the residents look forward to buying seeds for planting. In the summer, the people look forward to working outside among the sunflowers and repairing their fences. Appalachians long to sit in rockers on their porches

and look at the beautiful mountain view in the fall, and in the winter, they look forward to building fires and watching the hollows fill up with snow. The children love all the seasons and always seem to find something special to do in each one.

- Have you ever helped repair a fence? What do you look forward to most in the summer?
- When you stand outside your house, what do you see? Describe the view.
- What do you like most about winter?
- Have you ever helped plant a garden in the spring? What did you plant?
- What is your favorite season? Why?

2. The Appalachians in this story are described as feeling happy and free. They look forward with eagerness to what each season has to bring. Invite students to suggest why the Appalachians in this story seem so content.

- Why do you think the people in this story feel so happy?
- Would you like to visit Appalachia?
- How do you think the people living in Appalachia would feel if you came to visit them? Why?
- How would you feel if a new student joined our class?

3. Invite students to look closely at the cover of the book. Ask children what they notice about the surroundings. Help students point out characteristics throughout the illustrations in the story that depict a rural community. Help children compare a rural environment with an urban community.

- As you look at the pictures of Appalachia, what do you notice?
- Do you see any traffic lights, high-rise buildings, or traffic jams? Why not?
- Appalachia is known as a rural community because it does not have some of the things you would find in a big, busy city. What places do you know about or have visited that are like Appalachia?
- Would you rather live in a rural community or a big city? Why?

4. Coal is a black or brown solid substance that can be burned to provide heat. A coal miner's job is very hard and dangerous. The miners work underground breaking coal loose from the walls of the coal mines. The mountains in Appalachia are full of coal. Discuss mining with the children.

- What does a miner do?
- Why do you think people want coal?
- How would you describe the miner in the story illustration?
- Would you want to be a coal miner? Why or why not?
- Why do you think the miner in the story has a small light on his hat?

Extend Your Experience

As the Crow Flies

- butcher paper
- markers
- yarn

The mountains and hollows surrounding Appalachia make traveling difficult. "As the crow flies," meaning in a straight line, would be a much shorter distance to travel than would a winding path. Talk with children about why a mountainous road cannot be made into a straight line.

Divide the class into small cooperative groups and give each group a sheet of butcher paper. Invite children to mark point A on one end of the paper and point B on the other. Encourage students to draw a winding path spanning the distance from point A to point B. Have students measure the winding path using yarn. Then have students stretch another piece of yarn from point A to point B in a straight line. Invite the children to compare the two lengths of yarn.

Inspired Thinkers

- scenic rural pictures from books, magazines, or travel brochures

The story describes the people in Appalachia as being "thinkers"— quietly reflecting on their surroundings, but not often expressing their thoughts in words. Invite children to be "inspired thinkers" as well. Show children various scenic pictures and ask them what the scenes make them think about. Encourage students to express their thoughts about the scenes, including what the scenes remind them of or how the scenes make them feel.

Making Homemade Jelly

The aroma of tasty, home-cooked meals often wafts from the kitchens of the homes in Appalachia. Delicious fried chicken, flaky biscuits, fried squash, and sausage gravy are among some of the food favorites. A fitting gift for a newcomer to Appalachia might be a homemade treat, such as a cherry cobbler. Make a special treat with your class by filling hand-decorated jars with some homemade jelly to give away as gifts.

Homemade Jelly	
• 1 can (6 oz or 180 ml) frozen orange or grape juice concentrate, thawed	Stir juice, water, and pectin in a saucepan until the pectin is dissolved. Heat to a boil over high heat, stirring constantly (about 2
• 2 cups (500 ml) water	minutes). Add the sugar. Heat to a
• 1 pkg (1 ³/₄ oz or 52.5 ml) powdered fruit pectin	boil again, stirring constantly. Remove from heat. Immediately pour the mixture into hot, sterilized baby-
• 3 ³/₄ cups (930 ml) sugar	food jars and cover with lids. The jars can be stored in the refrigerator for
• baby food jars	no longer than two months.

When the jelly has cooled, give each child a jar to decorate with fabric scraps and ribbon. Students can cut a circle from fabric a bit larger than the lid and tie a ribbon around the neck of the jar to hold the fabric in place. Or, students can cut out small shapes from the fabric and glue the shapes on the sides of the jar. Encourage students to give their homemade gifts to friends or family members.

Seasons

- drawing paper
- markers or crayons

List the four seasons on the chalkboard. Encourage students to recall the activities the residents of Appalachia in the story enjoyed during each season. List the ideas under the correct seasonal names on the chalkboard.

Give each child a sheet of drawing paper. Invite students to choose their favorite season and write the name of that season at the top of the paper. Then ask the children to divide the sheet of paper in half by drawing a line down the middle. On one side of the paper, encourage children to draw a picture of people in Appalachia enjoying one of the activities listed on the chalkboard for that season. On the other half of the paper, invite students to draw a picture of themselves enjoying their favorite seasonal activity.

Star Boy

Retold and illustrated by Paul Goble
New York: Bradbury Press, 1983

Synopsis

Star Boy was born in the Sky World. The Sun and the Moon were his grandparents. As a boy, he lived on earth with a mysterious scar across his face. The people said the scar was the result of his mother's disobedience for which she and Star Boy were cast down to earth. Star Boy seeks the Sun's forgiveness in hopes that his scar will be removed and he will be free to marry his beautiful bride.

Background

The Blackfeet belong to a group of Native Americans known as the Plains Indians. Years ago, they lived in an area of tall mountains and flowing rivers that spread out from the Rocky Mountains in all directions. They adopted a nomadic way of life. Today, descendants of the Blackfeet live in Alberta, Canada and northwestern Montana.

Deepen Your Understanding

1. Long ago, the Blackfeet built very large and distinctive tipis (also spelled "teepees"). The framing poles of the tipis extended several feet above the tops of the skin covers. The tipis were often decorated with colorful designs which had special meanings. Invite children to notice the tipis illustrated in the story and compare

these homes to other homes they have seen. Be sure children realize that not all Native Americans lived in tipis. The type of shelter depended on the tribe's lifestyle and available materials for building. The Blackfeet lived in tipis because they moved frequently and the tipis were easy to carry and assemble.

- How are the homes you see in the story different from the home you live in?
- Why do you think the Blackfeet lived in tipis?
- Would you like to live in a tipi? Why or why not?

2. Some early Native American tribes used a type of cradle board to carry their babies, just like the girl in the story used to carry Star Boy. Cradle boards differed from tribe to tribe. A woman could strap the cradle board to her back or carry it in her arms. The cradle board made carrying the baby much easier. Sometimes the cradle board was even hung on a tree within sight to keep the baby from crawling away.

- Have you ever carried a baby? Was it hard?
- What are some ways you have seen people carry babies?
- Do you think using a cradle board would make carrying a baby easier? Why?

3. Many tribes who practiced the Sun Dance (which is mentioned in the story) did so for various reasons. It was seen as a method to come in contact with the Spirit World, renew nature, keep buffalo plentiful, bring victory into battle, and to settle quarrels. The dance could last from eight to twelve days and was seen as a test of endurance. Relate this Native American tradition with a marathon activity with which students may be familiar, such as a race, swimming, or a long ball game.

- Have you ever tried to do the same thing for a very long time? What happened?
- What kinds of dances do you like to do?
- What do you do when you get tired of dancing?

4. Star Boy asked the birds and animals for help as he tried to find his way back to the Sky World. He knew they had a different kind of wisdom. When Star Boy became too tired to continue, the path left for him by the two loons seemed to give him new energy. Help students understand the importance Native Americans place on nature and to think about the role nature plays in their own lives.

- Have you ever followed a path? What special signs showed you the way?
- What are some parts of nature you see, hear, or feel each day?
- How would your life be different if nature were not a part of your day?

- How do you help look after nature around you? Do you recycle at home? Can you pick up trash from your neighborhood?

Extend Your Experience

Star Gazing

- clean, empty soup cans
- masking tape
- aluminum foil
- rubberbands
- toothpicks
- flashlights

With such a beautiful view of the blanket of stars on a clear night, the Plains tribes naturally developed a strong interest in the "sky country." When they gazed at the night sky, they imagined what the stars could be. Some saw outlines of familiar animals and others imagined each individual star to be a person, animal, or object.

Students can make tin can planetariums and enjoy gazing at the stars right in the classroom. Give a clean, empty soup can that is open at both ends to each child. Put masking tape around the rims of the cans to eliminate any sharp edges. Place a piece of aluminum foil tightly over one end of each can and secure the foil with rubberbands. Using a toothpick, children can punch tiny holes in the aluminum foil to make constellation arrangements. Help students try to replicate an actual constellation, or design one of their own. Then show the children how to stick flashlights through the open ends of the cans and shine the starry arrangements they have created on the wall. Students can imagine what person, animal, or object the stars seem to form.

Sun Mosaics

- construction paper (orange, yellow, and white)
- scissors
- glue
- pencils

The Native Americans in the story recognized that the sun's rays provided light and warmth. Without the sun, nothing would grow. Students can make sun mosaics that resemble the striking illustration in the story when Star Boy returns to the Sky World to speak to the Sun.

Before beginning this project, use a paper cutter to make small rectangular pieces of orange, yellow, and white construction paper (3/4" x 1 1/2" or 2 cm x 3.8 cm). Give each child an assortment of these colorful rectangles. Help children use scissors to cut each small rectangle in half on a diagonal to make long narrow triangles. Invite children to glue the brightly colored triangles on a sheet of white or colored construction paper to form a beautiful round sun. Then encourage the children to create sentences expressing thanks to the sun just as Edgar Red Cloud did as recorded at the end of the story. Write the sentences on the sun mosaics. Display the sun mosaics on a bulletin board.

Tipis

- clay
- plastic straws or 9" (22.9 cm) dowels
- 6" x 15" (15.3 cm x 38.2 cm) strips of construction paper
- tape
- scissors
- crayons or markers

Tipis were made with long poles tied together at the top and spread out at the bottom. A semicircle of buffalo skins was placed over this structure. These Native American homes were often decorated with colorful designs which had significance among the tribes.

Invite students to construct small tipis. Have each child roll a lump of clay into a long snake and lay it on the desk or table top to form a 5" (12.7 cm) circle as the base of the tipi. Help children insert six straws or dowels (evenly spaced) around the clay base, angled in towards the center at the top. Give each student a 6" x 15" (15.3 cm x 38.2 cm) strip of construction paper. Help students find the center of one of the 15" (38.2 cm) sides. Using scissors, help students make a semicircle from the rectangle by gently rounding the corners along one 15" (38.2 cm) side. Students can start cutting from the center mark and arc up to each corner. Invite students to use crayons or markers to make colorful designs on the tipis. Then have students wrap the completed covers around the tipi frames and tape in place.

Marathon Moves

- kitchen timer

The Sun Dance required a lot of physical endurance by the dancers. Invite the children to brainstorm a list of physical activities that they think they could do for a long time, such as hopping on one foot, jogging, doing jumping jacks, skipping, jumping rope, and so on. Students might like to try doing these physical challenges together. Set a time limit, for example three to five minutes, and invite the children to join you in doing these exercises for a set amount of time. Help students understand how the Sun Dance participants might have felt when they became very tired and yet continued to dance. Explain to the children that they may not be able to do the exercises for the full amount of time and that it is okay if they need to stop.

The Story of Light

Written and illustrated by Susan L. Roth
New York: Morrow Junior Books, 1990

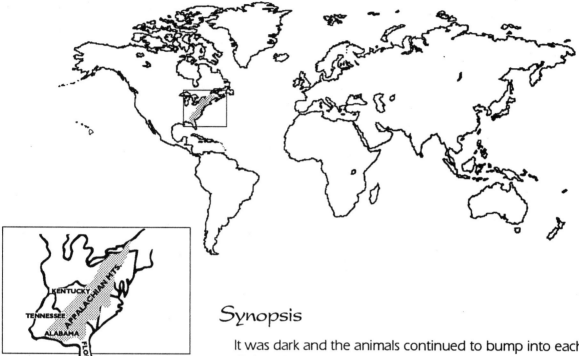

Synopsis

It was dark and the animals continued to bump into each other until they decided it was foolish to live in such darkness. All they needed to do was snatch a bit of the sun for themselves. In this Cherokee myth, the "smallest of voices" finally devises a plan that brings light to the darkened land.

Background

Creation stories are often found among tales told by indigenous people throughout the world. This story was inspired by a Cherokee tale. The Cherokee are one of the woodland tribes in the Appalachian Mountain territory. Variations of this tale of light can be found in other Native American legends.

Deepen Your Understanding

1. Just as in *The Story of Light*, it is common in Cherokee tales for animals to hold council meetings to solve problems. Discuss with children how they best solve problems. Compare and contrast students' problem-solving methods with the characters in the story.

    ▪ Have you ever discussed a problem with a group of friends? Did it help solve the problem?

- Would you rather solve a problem by yourself or ask others for help? Why?
- Have you ever argued with your friends when you were working together? How did you solve your problem?

2. Possum was given the big job of being first to try to snatch a bit of the sun to bring back to his fellow animal friends. Though he tried very hard, he was not able to do it.

- Why do you think the other animals agreed that Possum should be first to visit the sun?
- How do you think Possum felt as he neared the sun while squeezing his eyes tightly closed as the brightness burned closer?
- How do you feel when others are depending on you to do a job?
- What advice would you have given to Possum if he had tried a second time?

3. Many Cherokee legends are told to explain elements of nature. There are tales about how the animals got fire, why the raccoon has rings on his tail, how the deer got his horns, and why the owl has spotted feathers.

- Have you ever wondered why something is the way it is? What do you wonder about?
- What are some things you have noticed in nature that you cannot explain?
- Who do you ask when you don't know an answer?
- What would you do if no one could tell you the answer? How would you explain what you saw?

4. Spider was first seen in the story as not good enough for the job. However, her determination and self-confidence was rewarded with success. Encourage students to see the value in such characteristics.

- How do you think the animals' feelings toward Spider changed after she brought the sun to them?
- Have you ever changed the way you felt about someone or something? Why?
- Have you ever tried to prove to someone that you could do something they didn't think you could do? What happened?
- How are you like Spider? How are you different?

Extend Your Experience

Accepting Applications!

Cherokee legend says that long, long ago, animals mingled on equal terms with humans and spoke the same language. Review some of the animals' personality characteristics from the story.

Bear never thought too long about anything.
Wolf was a wanderer.
Buzzard thought he knew better.
Spider was small and viewed as not important.

As the story illustrates, legend claims that the animals held council meetings. Invite children to choose an animal they think would be perfect for the job of snatching a bit of the sun. Encourage students to assume the role of that animal and give a speech before the council persuading the others to let him or her do the job.

That Explains It

- *Cherokee Animal Tales* by James Mooney

In the story, the animals' journeys to the sun explain why they look and act as they do today. The Possum shuns the sun and has no fur on his tail. The Buzzard has no feathers on his head. The Spider's web looks like the sun's rays. There are other stories that explain the Possum's furless tail. Read "Why the Possum's Tail Is Bare" from *Cherokee Animal Tales* by James Mooney (see the bibliography on page 207). Compare the similarities and differences between the tales. Invite children to compose alternate legends as to why the Buzzard has no feathers on his head or why the spider's web looks like the sun's rays.

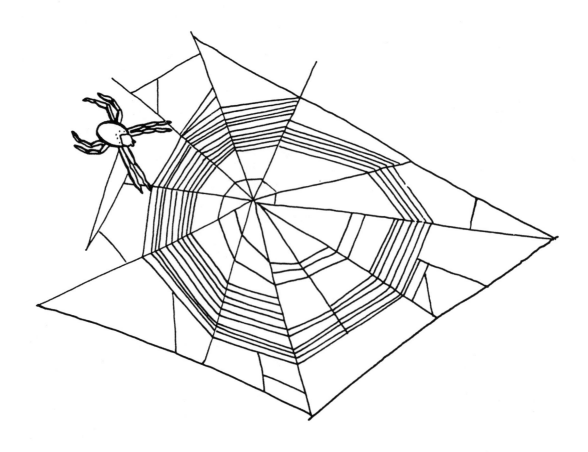

Coiled Clay Pots

- self-hardening clay
- rolling pins
- plastic knives
- plastic bags
- wet sponges
- sandpaper
- paint (optional)

The Cherokee make pottery from natural clay with a bit of sand added. Pots are made using the coil method and often decorated with serpents and sunflowers or painted with red and yellow paint.

Invite students to make their own pots using the coil method. Have each student flatten a clump of clay with a rolling pin to make a base for their pots. Help the children use plastic knives to trim the bases of their pots to the desired size. Next, children roll clumps of clay into flat slabs about 1/4" (.5 cm) thick. Cut the slabs into 1/2" (1.2 cm) strips. Have the children roll each strip gently under the palms of their hands until it is a smooth coil. Taper the coils at each end. (If the coils crack or break when they are manipulated, add more water to the clay.) Show the children how to wrap the coils from the base of the pot upward. About halfway up, moisten fingers with water and demonstrate how to smooth the clay both inside and out with the fingers. Have the children continue wrapping the coils around to complete the pot and then smooth the upper half with their fingers.

Just as the spider's pot grew harder and drier as she neared the sun, so clay pots today are still dried slowly. Place the clay pots in plastic bags with holes poked in them for slow drying. When the clay has hardened, the pots can be further smoothed and shaped with sandpaper. Designs can be etched in the clay with a pencil before the clay is hardened, or the children may paint their pots after the clay has dried.

Giver of Life

- two identical plants

The Cherokee, like other Native American tribes, look upon the sun as the giver of life. Invite students to brainstorm a list of things that need the sun to grow. Invite students to compare a plant's growth that receives sunlight to a plant's growth that does not. Place one plant in a dark environment and allow the other to sit in a sunny windowsill. Give both plants water and check on them regularly. Discuss with the children the differences in the growth of each plant.

Lion Dancer: Ernie Wan's Chinese New Year

Written by Kate Waters and Madeline Slovenz-Low and photographed by Martha Cooper
New York: Scholastic, 1990

Synopsis

Ernie Wan shares the wonder and excitement of the Chinese New Year with his family in New York. The celebration centers around Ernie's first Lion Dance performance.

Background

New Year's day is one of the happiest holidays of the year and is celebrated all over the world. The Chinese New Year comes on the first day of the lunar calendar, varying from January 21 to February 19. The Chinese get up early in the morning on New Year's Day. They exchange greetings and wishes with each other. They give thanks for a safe and happy year and wish for a prosperous year to come.

Deepen Your Understanding

1. Point out the emotions Ernie felt as he anxiously waited to perform his Lion Dance. Help children realize that children all over the world have similar emotions.

- Ernie was so excited, he had trouble sitting in school and taking a nap later that evening. Why was Ernie so excited?
- Have you ever been so excited that you couldn't sleep? Why?
- Ernie tells the story of the "most important day" in his life. Why was this day so important to him?
- What has been your most important day? Why?

2. Children in China often go to school six days a week. After the school day is over, some students go to a Children's Palace, often found in large cities, where they study dance, painting, or music. Ernie goes to a special school to learn to read and write Chinese. Later he goes to his father's school to learn kung fu.

- If you could study dance, painting, or music, which would you choose? Why?
- If you could go to a special school, what would you like to learn?
- Ernie thinks writing is the hardest to learn. What is the hardest thing for you to learn?

3. Family honor is important in the Chinese culture. Ernie's father told him that by doing the Lion Dance well, he would bring honor to the family. Talk about honor with the children.

- What do you think Ernie's father meant when he said that Ernie would bring honor to the family by doing the Lion Dance well?
- How do you think Ernie felt when everyone clapped and cheered at the end of the dance?
- Do you think Ernie brought honor to his family? Why?
- Have you ever brought honor to your family? How?
- What do you think you could do to bring honor to your family?

4. Ernie Wan explains many Chinese customs and traditions that are associated with the New Year celebration—wearing new clothes, giving and receiving red envelopes filled with money, and lighting firecrackers. Invite students to compare Ernie's celebration with their New Year's celebration activities.

- Have you ever done any of the things Ernie did to celebrate the New Year? What?
- What would you most like to do to celebrate the New Year?
- How do you celebrate the New Year?
- Why do you think people celebrate a new year?

Extend Your Experience

Language Lesson

Give children the opportunity to more closely identify with Ernie by trying to learn some Chinese words or sayings. Here are some useful phrases children can learn to say.

English	Chinese
How are you?	Ni hao (nee▪how)
Good-bye	Sai jian (sai▪jien)
Thank you	Xie xie (shei▪shei)
Please	Qing (cheeng)

Chinese Writing

- drawing paper
- black paint
- paintbrushes

Ernie went to a special school on Saturdays to learn to read and write Chinese. He found writing to be the hardest to learn. Students can try writing the Chinese characters for the numbers 1-10. Show the children how to draw each character using black paint and a brush. Model the strokes on an easel or chart in front of the room. Invite children to copy the strokes using paint, brushes, and paper at their desks.

i (yee) one

uhr (er) two

sahn (sahn) three

suh (suh) four

wu (woo) five

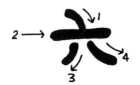

liu (leo) six

chi (chee) seven

ba (bah) eight

ju (jeo) nine

shur (shur) ten

Lai See

- 6" (15.3 cm) red construction-paper squares
- gold stickers
- gold glitter or gold pens

Uncle Jimmy gave Ernie a red envelope with money in it. These special red envelopes are called "lai see." The envelopes are often decorated with gold calligraphy. These envelopes are given to express good wishes.

Give each child a 6" (15.3 cm) red construction-paper square. Invite children to write or dictate special good luck wishes in the middle of one side of the squares. Help children fold up the corners of the squares to the center. Place gold stickers in the centers to secure all four corners and seal the messages. Encourage children to use gold glitter or gold pens to decorate the outsides of the special message envelopes. Collect all the completed messages and distribute them randomly. Invite children to open the envelopes and read their good luck wishes.

Lion Dance

- cardboard boxes
- long pieces of fabric or sheets
- crayons or markers
- glue
- collage materials

Closely examine the lion head Ernie used for his dance. Discuss some of its features. Divide the class into small groups of three or four. Invite each group to make a lion head using a cardboard box big enough to fit over a child's head. Encourage students to be creative and use a variety of materials, such as egg carton eyes, brightly colored strips of paper, and shiny glitter. After each group has made a lion's head, attach a long piece of cloth or a sheet that will cover several children. Invite parents to help with this project, if possible. Children will need some assistance and the project may extend over several days. After the projects are completed, encourage each group of children to perform their own Lion Dance. Be sure each child gets a chance to wear the lion head, just as Ernie did.

A Promise Is a Promise

Written by Robert Munsch and Michael Kusugak and illustrated by Vladyana Krykorka
Altona, Manitoba: D. W. Friesen & Sons, 1988

Synopsis

Allashua's mother warns her that Qallupilluit, who live under the sea ice, grab children who go near the ocean ice without their parents. Allashua promises to stay away from the ice, but has no intention of keeping her promise as she sets off to go fishing. Her encounter with the Qallupilluit changes her perspective about listening to her parents' warnings and knowing what it means to keep a promise.

Background

Inuit is the native name for the Eskimo. The Inuit live across the northern parts of Alaska and Canada. Michael Kusugak was born on the west coast of the Hudson Bay. Since the Inuit traditionally spent a lot of time on the sea ice, they invented the make-believe character called "Qallupilluit" as a means of keeping children away from dangerous crevices.

Deepen Your Understanding

1. Allashua promised to go fishing in the lake and not in the ocean. However, she soon broke her promise. Later, to get out of a tight spot, Allashua made another promise to the Qallupilluit, which she realized would be hard to keep. Invite children to relate their own experiences of making and keeping promises with Allashua's.

- Why do you think Allashua broke her promise to stay away from the ocean ice?
- Have you ever made a promise? What did you promise? Did you keep your promise?
- What do you think "a promise is a promise" means?
- Do you think Allashua will make any more promises? Do you think she will keep them?
- Have you ever had to keep a promise that you wish you had never made?

2. Allashua's family said she was "not so smart" to promise the Qallupilluit that she would bring her brothers and sisters to the ice. Her family also thought it was "not so smart" of her to call the Qallupilluit nasty names.

- Do you think Allashua would agree that some of the things she did were "not so smart"?
- Have you ever done something that was "not so smart"? What?
- What do you think would help you be "smart," rather than "not so smart"?
- Why do you think Allashua's parents told her not to do something?
- How would Allashua's day have been different if she had listened to her parents and kept her promise?
- Have you ever done something you were told not to do? What?

3. Allashua's fishing adventure turned out quite differently than she expected. Allashua's fishing experience is undoubtedly different than a fishing experience the children may have had. Invite students to compare fishing in the arctic with fishing in other places.

- Have you ever been fishing? Where?
- How was Allashua dressed to go fishing? How did you dress when you went fishing?
- What kind of fish do you think Allashua caught? What kind of fish have you caught? Were the fish you caught bigger than Allashua's? Or were they smaller?
- Allashua used a fishing pole. What other kinds of things can you use when you go fishing?

4. Allashua was wearing a parka, warm boots, and mittens on her fishing adventure. During the coldest part of the year, the temperatures in Alaska and Canada may be 10° F (-12° C) or below for many days of the year.

- If Allashua invited you to go fishing with her, what would you wear?
- What is the temperature on a winter day where you live?
- Which of your clothes would you probably never wear if you lived where Allashua and her family lived?

Extend Your Experience

What is a Qallupilluit?

- lined paper
- drawing paper
- crayons or markers
- pencils

The Qallupilluit were invented by the Inuit as a means of keeping small children away from dangerous crevices in the sea ice. Parents thought that if children believed in and were frightened by this creature, they would take their warnings more seriously. Invite children to brainstorm a list of dangerous things at school or home where they have been warned to be careful. Perhaps a teacher has reminded them not to run in the hallway at school or a parent has reminded them to cross the street with care. Challenge students to create a tale that includes a make-believe creature, such as the Qallupilluit, that would keep students from ignoring the safety reminders. Invite children to write or dictate their imaginative stories and then draw an illustration of their creatures. Make a class book of the stories and drawings.

Icy Activities

- ice cubes
- plastic cups
- salt
- tablespoons
- paper towels
- world map

The Inuit live in one of the coldest regions of the world. They have learned to live with the cold and icy surroundings. Except for three months of the year, the land remains frozen. Invite students to discover some interesting characteristics about ice. Ask students to predict what the answer will be to each of these three questions:

Is ice wet or dry?
Will an ice cube sink or float in water?
Will ice melt faster in plain water or salt (ocean) water?

Divide the class into small cooperative groups and invite each group to test their predictions. Ask children to touch a piece of paper towel to an ice cube and count to ten to determine if ice is wet or dry. (The paper will remain dry.) Then have students put an ice cube in a glass and pour water over it to see if the ice will sink or float. (Ice is lighter than water so the ice cube will float.) To test the last prediction, have children fill two glasses half full of water. To one glass, add a tablespoon of salt and stir well. Carefully drop an ice cube in each glass. Invite students to observe what happens over the next few minutes as the cubes melt. (The ice in salt water will take longer to melt because salt increases the buoyancy of the ice cube. The part of the ice cube that is above the water melts more slowly.) Show the children a world map and invite students to point to places on the map where they think the climate would be icy and cold.

Blanket Toss

- blanket
- stuffed animal or doll

The blanket toss is an old Inuit custom once used by hunters to help find animals. Fellow hunters would form a circle and each hold tightly to the edge of a blanket and stretch it taut. A single hunter would lie in the center of the blanket. The other hunters would toss the hunter up in the air by raising the blanket in unison. Invite your students to try this custom that has now become a game for Inuit children. (For safety reasons, toss a stuffed animal or doll in the air rather than a student!) Invite students to form a circle and hold tightly to the edges of the blanket. Place the stuffed animal or doll in the center and encourage children to toss and catch their "hunter."

Ice Fishing

- construction paper
- clear contact paper (or laminating machine)
- large paper clips
- magnets
- fishing line
- popsicle sticks
- clear plastic container
- scissors

Help children cut small fish from construction paper (about 2" or 5.0 cm long). Laminate the fish or cover both sides of the fish with clear contact paper. Slide a large metal paper clip over the mouth and down the body of each fish. Then fill the plastic container about two-thirds full of water and put the container in a freezer. Freeze the water until there is at least one inch of ice on the top. Remove the container from the freezer and poke a small fishing hole in the center of the ice. Invite children to drop the laminated fish into the water through the hole. Show the children how to make fishing poles by attaching magnets to one end of a piece of fishing line and attaching a popsicle stick to the other. Invite children to drop their "hooks" through the ice hole and try to catch some fish, just as Allashua did.

The Keeping Quilt

Written and illustrated by Patricia Polacco
New York: Simon & Schuster, 1988

Synopsis

When Great-Gramma Anna came to America, all that she had left from Russia were her dress and babushka. These later became scraps used to make a treasured quilt that has tied generations together for over a century. The "keeping quilt" is used as a wedding huppa, a baby blanket, a picnic blanket, and most importantly, to keep memories alive.

Background

Around the turn of the century, large numbers of Russian Jews fled the pogroms (riots against Jews) to come to America. Many came to this country with little money and few possessions. They brought both Eastern European and Orthodox Jewish traditions with them to their new homeland. Through cooking, storytelling, handicrafts, and religious observations, the immigrants were able to keep memories of "backhome Russia" alive.

Deepen Your Understanding

1. Wedding ceremonies around the world are filled with cultural traditions. In Jewish tradition, as illustrated in the story, the bride and groom stand beneath a canopy called a "huppa" (hup•puh). Jewish weddings often include the groom crushing a glass beneath his foot at the end of the ceremony. And, as mentioned

in the story, after some Jewish weddings, the men and women dance separately. Invite students to compare these wedding traditions with those with which they are familiar.

- Have you ever been to a wedding?
- What are some things you noticed happening at the wedding?
- Have you ever seen a huppa or canopy similar to the one in the story? Where? What was it used for?
- In what ways were the three weddings in the story alike? In what ways were they different? Why?

2. The "keeping quilt" was used for many purposes. But most importantly, it served as a means of keeping memories alive. It was handed down from generation to generation and used over and over again. As Patricia traced her finger around the edges of the quilt designs, her mother told her whose sleeve, apron, or dress had contributed the fabric for each patchwork piece.

- How would these families' lives be different if they had not had the "keeping quilt" to pass on to each other?
- Has anyone ever passed something on to you? What?
- Do you have any family photo albums? Do you like to look at them?
- When you get older, what would you like to pass on to someone else in your family? Why?

3. Families are a major theme in *The Keeping Quilt*. Not only are traditions and quilts passed down from generation to generation, but habits and values as well. For example, Carle learned to keep the Sabbath and to cook, clean, and do the washing from her mother. Encourage children to see the value in learning from older family members.

- Would you like to be part of the family in the story? Why or why not?
- How would you describe the families in the book? How would you describe your family?
- What have you learned to do from someone in your family? What do you think your parents learned from your grandparents?
- Is it important to learn from older family members? Why or why not?

4. Patricia Polacco's family emigrated from Russia to the United States. They came with very little money or possessions and probably left behind friends, family, and a way of life with which they were accustomed. Help students share and consider how it would feel to leave a familiar home and move to a new environment.

- How did Great-Gramma Anna's family change when they came to America? How do you think she felt about her new home?

- How do you think she felt when she left Russia? Why?
- Do you think it would be easy or hard to learn to speak and read a new language? Why?
- Have you ever moved to a new place? What was it like? How did you feel about it at first? Did you miss your friends? Did you make new ones?

Extend Your Experience

Making Challah

On Friday nights, Anna and her family would say the prayers of the Sabbath. Then the family would eat challah and chicken soup. Challah is a beautiful braided bread eaten on the weekly holy day. Invite students to help you prepare challah to enjoy together.

Challah	1
• 4 ½ to 5 ½ cups (1 ⅛ l to 1 ½ l) flour	Mix 1 ¼ cups (310 ml) flour, sugar, salt, and undissolved yeast. Add the
• 2 Tbsp (30 ml) sugar	margarine. Gradually add hot water.
• 1 ½ tsp (7.5 ml) salt	Beat two minutes on medium speed
• 1 pkg active dry yeast	with an electric mixer. Add 2 more cups
• ⅓ cup (90 ml) soft margarine	(500 ml) of flour, 3 eggs, and one egg white. Stir in enough additional flour to
• 1 cup (250 ml) hot tap water	make a soft dough. Knead the dough on a floured board for 15 minutes. Place
• 4 eggs (room temperature)	the dough ball in a well-greased bowl. Cover and let rise about 1 to 1 ½ hours.
• ¼ tsp (1.25 ml) poppy seeds (optional)	Then punch the dough down and divide the dough in half. Divide one of the halves into three equal pieces. Roll each

piece into a 12" (30.6 cm) strip. Connect the three strips at one end by pinching the ends together. Braid the dough strips into a twisted loaf. Repeat with the other half of the dough ball. Place both braided loaves on a greased baking sheet. Brush the loaves with the remaining egg yolk and sprinkle with poppy seeds. Allow both loaves to rise for about 1 to 1 ½ hours. Then bake the loaves at 400°F (200°C) for 30 minutes.

Coming to America

- world map
- push pins
- yarn
- name cards
- student photographs (optional)

The Keeping Quilt tells one family's story of leaving their home country and traveling to America. America is composed of Native

Americans and immigrants from countries all over the world. Americans have strong heritages from their original homelands. Invite children to find out about their "homelands" by asking parents or other family members where their ancestors came from. Display a world map on a bulletin board. Use pins and yarn to connect each child's name with the country of his or her origin. Invite students to bring in photographs of themselves and family members to display beside their name cards.

Patchwork Pieces

- quilts or photographs of them (optional)
- construction paper, felt, or fabric pieces
- crayons or markers
- scissors
- glue

If possible, invite children to bring in and share handmade quilts. If that's not possible, bring photographs to share. Encourage the owners of the quilts to share the significance of the fabrics and designs used. Discuss with your class how quilts are made. Then invite children to make a quilt to symbolize special memories they share as a class. For example, students could make an end-of-the-year quilt, a quilt that represents an important class event, or a quilt that celebrates a theme or holiday.

Give each child a 6" (15.3 cm) square of construction paper, felt, or fabric. Invite students to create a picture on the square using crayons, markers, paper or felt scraps, and glue. When all the patchwork pieces are complete, assemble the quilt on a bulletin board or wall. You might want to alternate a student-made square with a solid color square as you piece the quilt together. Encourage students to talk about their work and share their memories with the class.

Good Luck Tokens

- paper
- pencils

Throughout the story, good luck tokens are given to various family members. Gold was given for wealth, a flower for love, salt so life would have flavor, and a sprinkle of wine for laughter. Invite students to guess why each token meant what it did. Encourage students to think of something nice they would wish for one of their friends or family members, such as joy, friendship, happiness, or good health. Then ask children to think of something that would make a good token for their wishes. Invite students to bring their tokens to class and write or dictate who the tokens are for and what each token means. Students can share their writing or the children's descriptions can be displayed on a bulletin board.

Aekyung's Dream

Written and illustrated by Min Paek
San Francisco: Children's Book Press, 1988

Synopsis

A young Korean girl struggles with the adjustment of her recent move to the United States. Feeling inadequate in her ability to speak English and dealing with the teasing from her classmates, she dreams of the wisdom of one of Korea's most important rulers. (Text is in Korean and English.)

Background

Korea is a beautiful country on the eastern edge of Asia. This peninsula is known as the "Land of the Morning Calm" and is thousands of years old. The author, Min Paek, was born in Seoul, Korea and immigrated to the United States in 1973. This story was written in the hope that it might encourage other newcomers as they struggle to adjust to a new culture.

Deepen Your Understanding

1. Aekyung felt like she was always alone when she was at school and nobody played with her. Her classmates teased her for being different. Aekyung's mother advised her to ignore the mean behaviors. Help children understand how Aekyung must have felt by relating her experience to a time they may have felt alone or teased.

- Why do you think the children teased Aekyung and did not play with her?
- Have you ever been teased? How did it make you feel?
- How would you treat Aekyung if she came into our classroom tomorrow?
- What advice would you have given Aekyung if she told you she was being teased?

2. Aunt Kim brought Aekyung a fancy Korean dress when she came to visit. Although most Koreans wear clothing similar to ours, they still respect their family traditions and old Korean ways. Many Koreans wear traditional clothes on special holidays and family days. The dress Aunt Kim gave Aekyung is called a "hanbok" (hahn▪boke). It is a long skirt that straps around the ribs and goes all the way down to the feet. This high-waisted skirt is worn with a short jacket that has a long bow in front.

- Where do you think Aekyung will wear her new dress?
- Do you think Aekyung should wear her new dress to school? Why or why not?
- What do you wear when you want to dress up and look your best?
- Have you ever worn something that looked very different from everyone around you? How did you feel?

3. When Aekyung heard the birds singing, she wondered if they were singing in English or Korean. She finally realized that birds understood the languages of all people. She could greet them by saying "hello" in English or in Korean (on▪yúng). Challenge children to think of universal ways to communicate that could be understood by people of all languages (music, dance, sign language, emotions).

- What are some ways you could communicate with Aekyung if you did not speak Korean?
- What words would you want to learn first if you were going to learn Korean? Why?
- What are the first English words you would teach Aekyung? Why?

4. King Sejong was one of Korea's most important rulers. He was often called "Sejong the Great" and he ruled from 1419 to 1450. One of his greatest achievements was to invent the Korean way of writing. Today King Sejong and his Korean alphabet are honored with a special holiday on October 9.

- King Sejong was famous for inventing an alphabet. What would you like to be famous for?
- What do you think is the greatest thing you have ever done?
- Do you know of any other famous Americans that we have a special holiday for? Who? Why are they famous?

Extend Your Experience

Newcomers Welcome

After Aekyung felt more comfortable speaking English and felt accepted by her classmates, she wondered how she might help other newcomers. Divide the class into small groups. Invite each group to think of a way they could help a new classmate who was unfamiliar with their culture. Encourage groups to follow through on the ideas. If the group decides they would help the newcomer learn English, encourage students to consider which words they would teach first, how they would teach the words, and so on.

Mukung Flower

- tissue paper (white, pink, or lavender)
- green chenille stems
- scissors
- string or thread

Korea's national flower is the Mukung flower, also known as the rose of Sharon. It is a type of hibiscus that blooms on a small, shrublike tree. The flowers vary in color and can be white, pink, or lavender. Invite children to make Mukung flowers using tissue paper and chenille stems. Invite each child to cut three different-sized circles from a single color of tissue paper. The largest circle should be about 5" (12.7 cm) in diameter and the edges of the circles should be cut in a wavy design. Have students place the three circles on top of each other with the largest circles on the bottom. Help each child push a green chenille stem up through the center of the circles (the largest circle first). Then show the children how to bring the circles up over the ends of the stems and tie the bottoms of the circles tightly to the stems with string. Encourage children to fluff the circles to form flowers.

To extend this activity, ask the children to find out what their state flower looks like and compare it with the Mukung flower. Invite students to make their state flower using similar materials.

Alphabet Celebration

- paper
- pencils

The Korean alphabet, made up of 14 consonants and 10 vowels, is called "hangul" (HAN•guhl). Because hangul is considered one of the most logical writing systems in the world, it is also one of the easiest to learn. Today, King Sejong and the alphabet he invented are honored every October 9 on Hangul Day. Invite children to join in the celebration of the Korean alphabet by learning to write the word "hello" in Korean.

Doesn't Anybody Know About Koreans?

- fairy tale
- birthday candle
- instant noodle cup

Aekyung was frustrated because no one seemed to know anything about Koreans. One classmate thought Aekyung was Chinese. Share some interesting pieces of information with your class about Koreans using the props listed.

- Read the opening of a fairy tale that begins with, "Once upon a time . . ." Tell students that although many of our make-believe stories begin with those words, in Korea, make-believe stories begin, "When tigers smoked long pipes . . ."
- Hold up the birthday candle and ask students how old a baby is on its first birthday. Explain to children that Korean babies are considered one year old at birth, so at the first birthday party, they are two years old. If you and a Korean child were born on the same day, the Korean child would be a whole year older than you!
- Hold up the instant noodle cup. Explain to the children that they may have eaten a very popular Korean dish called "ramyon." Ramyon is a noodle dish with a special flavoring. In Korea, it is made fresh, but it is also dried and packaged as an instant food for sale in other countries. It is easily prepared with boiling water.

Invite students to learn more about Korea by reading books or talking with friends and family members. Encourage students to share their discoveries with the class.

Family Pictures

Stories by Carmen Lomas Garza as told to Harriet Rohmer
San Francisco: Children's Book Press, 1990

Synopsis

This collection of pictures portrays the life of a family living in a Hispanic community in Texas. The author fondly recalls her childhood memories of birthday piñatas, making tamales, watching a curandera cleanse a sick neighbor, and sitting on the rooftop with her sister gazing at constellations. (Text is in Spanish and English.)

Background

Mexican-American families in the southwestern United States have many things in common with families living in Mexico. The mild climate allows for lots of outdoor activities and families can raise much of their own food, as portrayed in the story. Carmen Lomas Garza uses her artistic talents, which were cultivated by daily practice and her mother's inspiration, to provide readers with a glimpse into her own family life.

Deepen Your Understanding

1. Carmen Lomas Garza has many fond memories of her family. The family unit is a valued one in the Hispanic community, as it is in other cultures. The family provides support for one another in many ways and family members simply enjoy spending time together in celebration and relaxation.

- What do you enjoy doing with your family?
- Have you ever done some of the same things the author did with her family? What?
- How is the author's family different from yours? How is it the same?
- When does your family get together? What do you and your family do when you get together?

2. The Mexican custom of Las Posadas is so named because "posada" means "inn" or "lodging" in Spanish. The celebration traditionally begins on December 16 and continues on each of the nine evenings before Christmas. The procession is led by children or young adults bearing statues of the holy family or dressed like them. They go to a different house each night, singing the traditional song, "La Litania," in which Joseph asks for a room at the inn. Finally the family and whole procession are admitted to the house where a party is held. Children might also enjoy reading the story *Nine Days to Christmas* by Marie Hall Ets (see the bibliography on page 206).

- Do you celebrate Christmas?
- In what ways do you celebrate Christmas?
- What do you think happened at the party, once the travelers were invited to come inside?
- What are some of the things you and your family do at a Christmas party?

3. The author recalls a curandera (koo▪ran▪DEH▪ruh) visiting a neighbor to help heal her of the flu. Curandera(o) is a Spanish word which means "one who heals." Curanderas are different from doctors who work in hospitals. Doctors rely on medicine and surgery for healing. A curandera relies on home remedies and faith.

- Who helps you get well when you are sick?
- Do you know anybody who is famous for his or her ability to help and heal people?
- How is a curandera(o) like a doctor? How is he or she different from a doctor?
- Don Pedro Jaramillo (1829-1907) was a well-known curandero in Mexico. Can you find information about this honored healer?

4. The author painted a family picture of her sister and herself up on the roof talking about the future. Discuss with students that children all over the world dream of what their futures hold. Invite students to share dreams they have for their futures.

- What would you like to be when you grow up?
- What do you think you will have to do for that dream to come true?
- What did the author mean when she said that her mother "inspired" her to be an artist?
- Who inspires you to dream?

Extend Your Experience

Making Tamales

One of the special memories of the author is making tamales with her family. Make tamales together as a "classroom family."

Tamales	1
• corn husks (or aluminum foil)	Soak the corn husks in very hot water for about 15 minutes until they are
• 3 cups (750 ml) masa harina (prepared flour for making tortillas)	pliable. Remove any silk and then wrap in a towel to dry. (Aluminum foil may be used instead of husks.) To make the
• 1 cup (250 ml) shortening	dough, cream the shortening and add 1 ½ cups (375 ml) masa harina and salt.
• 2 cups (500 ml) chicken broth	Beat well. Add the chicken broth and the rest of the masa harina. Beat until
• 1 tsp (5 ml) salt	fluffy. When beaten sufficiently, a small
• 3 cups (750 ml) cooked chicken	ball of dough will float in water. Spread a thick layer of this masa dough inside
• 3 cups (750 ml) mild salsa	each husk or piece of foil. Put a generous spoonful of salsa on the masa dough

2

and spread it evenly. Add pieces of chicken to the center of the dough. Fold the tamales up like packages. Wrap the foil or husk around the tamales and tie each tamale with a corn husk strip. Place the tamales in a steamer for about 1 ½ to 2 hours. The pot must be deep enough to hold about 2" (5.0 cm) of water below the rack on which the tamales are placed. Continue to add water during the steaming time to be sure the pot does not run dry. When the tamales are cooked, the dough will come away from the husk or foil. Unroll the husks and enjoy!

Family Pictures

- construction paper
- crayons or markers
- lined paper
- pencils

Invite children to make a booklet of their own family pictures. Each child can draw some special family scenes on construction paper and staple the pictures together in a booklet. The family pictures may include preparing dinner, celebrating a holiday, playing together, and so on. Add a sheet of writing paper between pictures so children can write about or dictate what is happening in each scene. Encourage children to recognize similarities and differences between their families and Carmen Lomas Garza's family.

Papel Picado

- black construction paper
- scissors
- white butcher paper
- glue

The author used a traditional Mexican folk-art technique to make the small black and white pictures on each text page in *Family Pictures*. Images were cut in black paper using an X-acto knife. Give each child a 4 1/2" x 6" (11.4 cm x 15.3 cm) piece of black construction paper. Have each child fold the paper in half twice in the same direction. Invite children to cut shapes from both long edges, and then unfold the paper to see the cut designs. Mount the black designs on a large piece of white butcher paper displayed on a wall or bulletin board entitled, "Papel Picado."

Cookie Walk

- chalk
- cookies
- music
- basket or bag
- small slips of paper
- pencil

The author recalls playing a game known as a "cakewalk." The game was played as a way to raise money for students to attend the university. Give your students an opportunity to play a similar game using cookies. With chalk, draw a figure similar to the one in the story on the blacktop or play area. Be sure there is a numbered square for each player. Invite each child to stand on a number. Write each number on a small slip of paper and place the slips in a basket or bag. Start the music and invite students to walk in a clockwise direction around the circle. When the music stops, each student must be standing on a number. Draw one slip of paper from the basket or bag and read the number aloud. The student standing on that number receives a cookie. Continue the game giving all the students an opportunity to walk for a cookie!

Hello, Amigos!

Written by Tricia Brown and photographed by Fran Ortiz
New York: Henry Holt and Company, 1986

Synopsis

Frankie Valdez, a young Mexican-American boy, lives with his family in San Francisco. Frankie rides the bus to school, plays with his best friend, and goes to the Boy's Club in his neighborhood. But today is special. Today is Frankie's birthday. He looks forward with eager anticipation to his birthday fiesta that evening, complete with a mariachi band, a piñata, and guacamole.

Background

Like many other cultures, members of a Mexican-American family and the larger community family are a cohesive and supportive group. The traditions of the rich Mexican culture are preserved by those who have now made this country their home.

Deepen Your Understanding

1. Invite children to recall some of the things that made Frankie's birthday so exciting and special (classmates surprised him with a cake and a crown, had favorite foods at dinner, broke a piñata, and listened to mariachi music). Encourage children to compare Frankie's party with their own ideas of what their birthday celebrations would include.

- What part of Frankie's birthday fiesta would you have liked the most? Why?
- What three things would you want to happen at your birthday party?
- How would your birthday party be different from Frankie's? How would it be the same?

2. Frankie admitted that he sometimes doesn't understand his math lesson at school. He likes English best when he gets the right answer and he sometimes falls asleep during science movies. He enjoys sitting by his best friend, Marvin Martinez, and he loves to play outside. Help children realize that although Frankie may speak a different language, he shares similar emotions and experiences.

- What is your favorite subject in school?
- Frankie sometimes didn't understand math. What do you have trouble understanding?
- What game do you like to play at recess?
- How is Frankie's school day like yours? In what ways is it different?

3. After helping his best friend, Marvin Martinez, fix the sling for his broken arm, Frankie decided he might like to be a doctor when he grows up. Encourage students to share what they would like to be when they grow up. Promote the importance of a good education by discussing what it will take to achieve those dreams.

- What would Frankie have to do to become a doctor?
- Do you think Frankie will be a doctor when he grows up? Why?
- What would you like to be when you grow up? Why?

4. Frankie had many people in his life who were there to help him. His teacher, Mrs. Giddings, helped him understand math. His older brother and sister helped him do his homework. Frank, the program director at the Boy's Club, helped him learn to play pool. And, most importantly, his family helped him celebrate his birthday. Frankie was also a helper when he fixed his best friend's sling for his broken arm. Help children recognize the helpers in their lives and ways they can be a helper to others.

- How would Frankie have felt if Mrs. Giddings wasn't there to help him when he didn't understand his math? What would he have done?
- How would Frankie learn how to play pool if Frank did not teach him?
- What would Frankie's birthday celebration have been like without his family?
- Who are the people who help you in your life? How do they help you?
- Who do you help? How?

Extend Your Experience

Making Guacamole

Frankie and his family enjoyed some of their favorite Mexican foods for Frankie's birthday fiesta. Invite children to tell what favorite foods they would like to have at their birthday parties. Encourage children to try one of Frankie's favorites—guacamole. There are many ways to prepare this popular food, but the main ingredients are avocados and lime or lemon juice. (Without the fruit juice, the avocados turn brown quickly.)

Guacamole	
• 2 large avocados	Cut the avocados in half lengthwise and
• 1 small tomato (chopped)	remove the pits. Peel and cut the avocados into small pieces. Mash the avocados with
• ½ small onion (chopped)	a fork and blend with the other ingredients. Serve with tortilla chips or raw vegetables.
• 1 to 3 canned green chilies (chopped)	
• 1 Tbsp (15 ml) lime or lemon juice	
• ³/₄ tsp (3.75 ml) salt	
• tortilla chips or raw vegetables	

Birthday Bingo

- construction paper
- tagboard
- bingo markers (beans, macaroni, or paper clips)

Frankie and his family speak Spanish at home, but at school Frankie learns English. Like all children, Frankie feels happy and proud when he gets the answers right. Help children understand what it would be like to learn a new language by playing Spanish Birthday Bingo.

Before beginning this activity, make one paper birthday crown. Then, give each child a tagboard bingo card with nine squares. Write the birthday item words on page 79 on the board in English. Invite children to draw a picture of each item in one square of their bingo cards. Students should draw their pictures in random order so that each child's bingo card is different. Give children the Spanish word for each item drawn on their bingo cards. To begin the game, call out the name of one of the birthday items in Spanish. Invite students to find that picture on their cards and cover it with a marker (bean, macaroni, paper clip). The first student who covers three pictures in a row calls out "Feliz Cumpleaños." If the child is correct, he or she can wear the birthday crown. Clear the cards and play again. Each new winner can wear the birthday crown until a new winner is determined.

English	Spanish
game	juego (HWAY•go)
cake	torta (TOR•tah)
crown	corona (cah•ROH•nah)
candles	candela (cahn•DEL•ah)
party	fiesta (fee•ES•tah)
candy	dulces (DOOL•say)
gift	regalo (ray•GAL•oh)
ice cream	helado (hay•LAH•thoh)
balloon	globo (GLOH•boh)

Piñata Party

- large balloon
- newspaper strips
- wheat paste (or white glue and starch)
- pin
- scissors
- candy or small toys
- tempera paint
- paintbrushes
- crepe paper
- tape
- string
- plastic bat

A piñata is a decorated container filled with candies and toys. Traditionally, piñatas were made of clay, but now are often made of papier-mâché. Piñatas are often animal-shaped and decorated with crepe paper. For your piñata party, you can easily obtain an inexpensive piñata at a party supply store or children can make their own piñata from a balloon and papier-mâché.

Blow up a large balloon and tie a knot around the neck. Invite the children to cover the balloon with newspaper strips dipped in wheat paste or a mixture of glue and starch. Allow the balloon to dry completely. Pop the inner balloon by sticking a pin through the papier-mâché. Cut a small "door" in the piñata to insert candy or small toys. Tape the door closed and invite students to decorate the piñata using paint and crepe-paper streamers. Then enjoy a piñata party with the children. Suspend the piñata and give each student a couple of chances to break it. Remind children to share all of the goodies that fall once the piñata is broken.

Mariachi Band

- mariachi music

Mariachi bands are groups of strolling musicians that are commonly a part of holidays and special occasions in the Mexican culture. Instruments included in such a band are trumpets, marimbas, maracas, guitars, and violins. Frankie and his family enjoyed listening to mariachi music at Frankie's birthday party. Give your students an opportunity to do the same. There are many excellent records and tapes of mariachi bands available at your local library. Invite children to clap their hands and move their bodies to the music as they enjoy the lively sounds.

Iktomi and the Ducks

Retold and illustrated by Paul Goble
New York: Orchard Books, 1990

Synopsis

Iktomi, the trickster of Plains Indian folklore, devises a plan that he hopes will result in a delicious meal of roast duck. But with some unexpected distractions and the antics of the equally cunning Coyote, Iktomi ends up biting off more than he can chew.

Background

The Dakota Indians, also called the Sioux, are one of many Native American tribes known as Plains Indians. Paul Goble heard his first story about Iktomi, the trickster of Indian folklore, from Edgar Red Cloud while visiting Pine Ridge in South Dakota.

Deepen Your Understanding

1. In the story, Iktomi pretended to be either Sitting Bull or Crazy Horse. Sitting Bull is one of the most famous chiefs of the Western Sioux. He is admired for his courage, generosity, and loyalty. Crazy Horse was an equally courageous Sioux warrior. Invite children to compare these Native American heroes with people they admire.

   - Why do you think Iktomi wanted to be Sitting Bull or Crazy Horse?

- Have you ever pretended to be someone else? Who? Why?
- Sitting Bull and Crazy Horse are both heroes to the Sioux. Who do you think is a hero? Why?

2. The story begins with Iktomi looking for his horse. The early Native Americans placed a high value on horses. In fact, a family's wealth was often determined by how many horses they had. So, Iktomi was searching for something that was of great value to him. Encourage children to consider what they value and what would be worth searching for if they lost it.

- Have you ever lost something that was very special to you? What did you do?
- What is the most special thing you own?
- Why do you think horses were so important to the early Native Americans?
- Do you think Iktomi will ever find his horse? Why or why not?

3. Iktomi wanted to feel important. He wanted to ride in a parade so that everyone could see him in his magnificent clothes. He wanted everyone to notice him and admire his bravery. He wanted to pretend to be a famous Native American hero.

- Why do you think Iktomi wanted to feel important?
- What makes you feel important?
- Have you ever done something just so that you would be noticed? What?
- What famous hero would you like to pretend to be? Why?

4. Many Native American tales, as well as tales from many other cultures, provide explanations of the natural environment. In this story, ducks that have red eyes are said to be relatives of the ducks that peeked when Iktomi told them not to open their eyes. Legends and myths are an integral part of early tribal organization. There is a story for nearly everything the early Native Americans did. Every act of daily life had its own tradition.

- How does the story explain why some ducks today have red eyes? Do you think this is true?
- Why do you think the early Native Americans told stories about things they noticed in nature?
- Have you ever wondered why animals, trees, or people look the way they do?
- Have you ever tried to think of a way to explain something you saw?

Extend Your Experience

Tricksters

- lined paper
- pencils

Many Native American tribes have a trickster character like Iktomi. In some tribes, it was a spider, a coyote, or a raven. Stories about tricksters are tales called "ohunkaka" by the Lakota. These stories are not meant to be believed, but they often have a moral woven throughout them. The stories often illustrate human weaknesses or faults. The stories were told to help children overcome such weaknesses. Help students distinguish reality from make-believe in this tale about Iktomi.

Invite students to create their own stories that have similar elements as in *Iktomi and the Ducks*. For example, students must first decide on who will be their trickster character. Suggest that students all begin their stories in the same way, just as each Iktomi story begins with "(Trickster's name) was walking along. He (or she) was looking for . . ." Then students can create stories that explain a part of nature or present a lesson or moral value. Encourage students to be imaginative as they write. Invite students to share their stories with the class or "publish" the vignettes in a class book. Or, you may want to write a class story. Discuss the story ideas with the children. Write the story on the board as it is discussed and dictated. Then read the finished story aloud.

Decorative Pouch

- tan felt
- spray starch
- iron
- scissors
- tempera paint
- paintbrushes or cotton swabs
- hole punch
- yarn

Although Iktomi carried his bundle of grass by slinging a loaded blanket over his shoulder, the Plains Indians often carried their belongings in a carrying case called a "parfleche." A parfleche was made from a rectangular piece of rawhide that was folded up like an envelope. The case was most always painted with large, bold, geometric designs. A smaller, similar version was called a "pouch." Invite students to make decorative pouches.

Prepare a 12" x 18" (30.6 cm x 45.9 cm) piece of tan felt for each child by stiffening it with spray starch before ironing it. Shape the top of the felt piece to look like an envelope flap by cutting off two corners. Invite each child to use tempera paints to decorate the outside of the pouch with bold geometric designs. The simple geometric designs painted by the Native Americans were red, yellow, blue, green, brown, or black. After the paint has dried, fold each felt piece and punch four pairs of fringe holes on each side. Have children insert a 6" (15.3 cm) piece of yarn that has been folded in half through each hole in the pouches. Pull the loose ends through the loops. Repeat with each remaining hole to close up the sides of the pouches.

Bead Designs

- small macaroni
- food coloring
- rubbing alcohol
- newspaper
- bowls
- strong string
- adding machine tape
- construction paper
- scissors
- glue
- crayons or markers

Iktomi was dressed in his best clothes the day he set out to find his horse and ride in a parade. His outfit included a red silk shirt, moccasins, and beaded cuffs. The Plains Indians are known for their beautifully decorated clothing and bead work. They sewed rows of beads on everything from belts to moccasins. For this activity, use macaroni in place of beads.

Steep the macaroni in a bowl of 1 part food coloring to 10 parts rubbing alcohol. Dye the macaroni in a well-ventilated area and keep the alcohol mixture out of children's reach. Dye the macaroni different colors, if possible. Drain and spread the macaroni on newspaper to dry. Invite children to use the "beads" to create their own interesting clothing accessories. Students can make necklaces or chokers by stringing the macaroni or make cuffs using construction paper and gluing macaroni beads around the edges. Or, students can glue macaroni beads to headbands or belts made with adding machine tape. Encourage students to be creative. Have a parade of your own and invite children to model their accessories.

Pow-Wow Dance

- music (preferably Native American origin)

Iktomi told the ducks that he was on his way to a pow-wow to sing his new songs. He said that everyone would want to dance to his songs. Traditionally, pow-wows were celebrations of a particular event, such as the coming of spring, planting time, or harvest time. A pow-wow today is like a homecoming or a dance where old friends get together to celebrate. The round dance often starts off a pow-wow. Invite your students to try this simple dance.

Dancers stand in a circle and sidestep clockwise. To begin a sidestep, a dancer starts with feet together and then lifts the left foot off the ground and replaces it several inches to the left. The foot should be pointing straight down with the toe touching the ground. The dancer brings the heel down sharply while sliding the ball of the right foot into position next to the left. The dance repeats stepping to the left. To reverse the dance and move in a counterclockwise motion, the dancer begins the sidestep with the right foot. No particular costume is needed to perform this dance, but it is best done to music.

Quail Song

Adapted by Valerie Scho Carey and illustrated by Ivan Barnett
New York: G.P. Putnam's Sons, 1990

Synopsis

Quail cries "ki-ruu, ki-ruu" when a sharp blade of grass cuts her. Coyote thinks Quail's cry of pain is a beautiful song. He threatens to swallow her up if she does not teach it to him. To avoid becoming Coyote's meal, Quail teaches Coyote to cry as she did. But in the end, Coyote gets a taste of his own medicine.

Background

The name "pueblo" comes from the Spanish word for town or village. The people who live in these villages are called Pueblo Indians. There are many distinct groups of Native Americans included in this term, such as Hopi and Zuñi. The Pueblo Indians occupied the southwest part of the United States, including parts of Arizona, New Mexico, Utah, Colorado, and Nevada. About thirty pueblos are still inhabited today. The author's interest in Native American folktales inspired this original retelling of a Pueblo Indian tale.

Deepen Your Understanding

1. In the story, Quail was gathering grass seed for the winter. The Pueblo Indians also harvested and gathered their corn, bean, and squash crops to store for the winter or for the future. The Pueblo

Indians were outstanding farmers and their survival depended on their ability to raise crops in a very dry land.

- Have you ever tried to grow something? What happened?
- What do you think crops need to grow well?
- Do you have a garden? What do you grow in the garden?
- If you don't have a garden, what would you like to grow if you did?

2. The Hopi were considered the best musicians of all the Pueblo Indians. They were song makers by nature and actually sold songs to other Native Americans. Most Native American music is functional and always serves a purpose. Some songs were used to appeal for rain, some to help cure the sick, and some to honor heroes.

- Why do you think Coyote thought Quail's cry was a song?
- Why do you think Coyote liked the noise?
- What sound do you make when you are hurt? Does that noise ever sound like a song?
- What is your favorite song? Why?
- Why do you sing songs?

3. Much of the land in the Southwest is hot, dry desert. And, while most of the land is rocky or sandy, the landscape is described as being truly beautiful. One of the most beautiful times of day is at sunrise or sunset. The sun casts rays over the countryside and forms different colors and patterns. Invite students to compare and contrast the landscape depicted in the story with the area in which they live.

- Would you like to live in the southwestern United States? Why or why not?
- What colors do you see in the story illustrations? What colors do you see in nature where you live?
- How often does it rain where you live? How often do you think it rains where Quail and Coyote live? Why?

4. Quail distracted Coyote by painting eyes on a rock that was just her size. She fooled Coyote into thinking the decoy was actually her. Explain to the children what a "replica" is. Encourage students to compare and contrast what is real and what is a replica. Invite students to share replicas they have seen of "real" things.

- Why do you think Coyote was fooled by Quail's decoy?
- Would you have been fooled if you had been Coyote? Why or why not?
- In what ways were Quail and the painted rock alike? How were they different?
- Have you ever seen a replica of something? What? Did it look just like the real thing?
- If you were going to make a decoy of yourself, what materials would you use? Do you think you might be able to fool someone into thinking the decoy was really you? Why or why not?

Extend Your Experience

Coyote Tales

- *Doctor Coyote* by John Bierhorst

Just as Coyote is a central character in *Quail Song*, so is he an important figure in many Native American stories. The Coyote often plays the role of a trickster displaying his clever and witty ways. Coyote is an animal, but talks and acts like a human. He has great powers and he likes to be admired. But Coyote is not to be trusted. The Aztec Indians retold some of Aesop's fables using Coyote as the chief character. Share some of these Native American Aesop's fables with your class by reading John Bierhorst's *Doctor Coyote* (see the bibliography on page 206).

Southwest Mural

- butcher paper
- colored chalk
- paint
- crayons or markers

The landscape of the southwestern United States is composed primarily of sand and rocks. Near the river areas there is lush green growth. But the barren areas are home to plants and animals that do not need much water to survive, such as cacti, lizards, and snakes. The bright cactus blooms and the soft earth tones add to the beauty of the Southwest.

Divide the class into small cooperative groups and give each group a large piece of butcher paper on which to make a Southwest mural. Using information provided in this resource, illustrations from the story, and additional sources from your library, help children make a list of features of the natural environment in the Southwest. Encourage students to plan how they will make a mural that depicts the Southwest flavor. For example, students may start by making a sandy desert floor with clumps of grass and cacti in bloom. Students may also draw rock formations showing plateaus and canyons. The rock formations can be illustrated using earth tone colors with tints of purple, yellow, or light red. Invite students to add a village atop a plateau or some wildlife in the canyon. And the final touch might be to add a beautiful blue sky with billowy white cloud formations.

Pueblo Baskets

- construction paper
- crayons or markers
- plastic baggies

Most pueblo baskets contain some type of geometric design, zigzags, dots, or bands. Invite students to create a game using baskets. Give each student two small basket-shaped pieces of construction paper (identically shaped). Invite each student to decorate both of his or her baskets so that the pair of baskets look identical. Place six or seven pairs of paper baskets in small plastic baggies and make the sets available at a center. Encourage students to play a game of concentration with a partner using a set of decorated baskets. The players empty the baskets from the baggie and lay them face down. Each player in turn flips over two baskets to try to make a match. If the baskets match, the player takes them and continues by turning over two more. If the baskets do not match, they are turned back over and the player's turn is complete. The player with the most matches wins the game.

Rock Painting

- small flat rocks
- paintbrushes or cotton swabs
- tempera paint
- clear spray varnish

Quail painted a rock to act as a decoy, but Pueblo Indians also painted rocks for other reasons. Rocks were an appropriate "canvas" for painting because they were plentiful in the Southwest. Sometimes the Pueblo Indians painted directions on rocks. Sometimes they painted a picture on a rock of something they considered important, such as a corn stalk. Corn stalks were considered the "staff of life" because the crop was an important food source. Give students an opportunity to do some rock painting.

Begin collecting rocks several weeks before you begin this activity. Encourage students to bring rocks they have gathered from their yards. Invite students to paint a rock to look like a decoy. Or, students can paint a picture on the rock of something they consider to be important. Allow the painted rocks to dry. Spray the art pieces with clear varnish to seal and protect them.

Angel Child, Dragon Child

Written by Michele Maria Surat and illustrated by Vo-Dinh Mai
Milwaukee: Raintree Publishers, 1983

Synopsis

A young Vietnamese girl peeks around the corner as she enters her new American school for the first time. Without the support of her mother, who remains in Vietnam, Nguyen Hoa faces the challenges of the unfamiliar. Ut's biggest challenge is to tell her story to Raymond, a boy with fire-colored hair and a less-than-accepting attitude. Raymond ends up being instrumental in helping bring Ut's mother to the United States.

Background

Many Vietnamese have settled in the United States from 1975 to the present. Michele Maria Surat created this story after a Vietnamese child shared a photograph of her mother. The author hoped to create a book that would increase understanding and appreciation between American and Vietnamese children.

Deepen Your Understanding

1. Vietnamese write their last name first to emphasize the importance of the family. There are only about 30 family names for all Vietnamese. The most common family name is Nguyen (when•hwa) which is used by almost half of the population. The Vietnamese bow their heads to show respect and honor. They are not accustomed to the casual "hi" Americans use to greet one

another. Ut greeted the children in her class in the way she was familiar—she bowed and said, "chao buoi sang."

- How is Ut's name different from yours?
- Ut was Hoa's "at-home" name. Do you have a nickname?
- Why do you think the other children "screeched like bluejays" when they heard Ut's greeting the first day of school?
- Would you have reacted the same way? Why or why not?
- If you had been in Ut's classroom that first day of school, what would you have done to help Ut feel more comfortable?
- Have you ever been in a situation like Ut where you didn't understand what was going on around you? How did you feel? What did you do?

2. A Vietnamese legend claims that Vietnam's first king, who was the son of an Angelic Fairy, married the daughter of a noble Dragon King. Because of this, Vietnamese people are said to be descendants of both an Angelic Fairy and a Dragon King. As described in *Angel Child, Dragon Child*, the Vietnamese like to believe they have both sensitive and determined spirits.

- How do you think an angel acts?
- How do you think a dragon acts?
- How did Ut act like an angel child?
- When did Ut act like a dragon child? What caused her to act that way?
- Do you act most often like an angel child or a dragon child? Why?

3. Many things were new and different for Ut when she came to America. People dressed differently, talked differently, and acted differently. Places looked unfamiliar and even the weather was different. Encourage children to imagine what it might have been like to be in Ut's or Raymond's position.

- Why do you think Raymond was so mean to Ut in the beginning of the story?
- Why do you think Raymond started treating Ut differently after a while?
- How were Raymond and Ut different from one another? How were they alike?
- Do you think Raymond and Ut will continue to be friends?
- How are your friends different from you?

4. Raymond teased Ut and her sisters the first day of school because they were wearing clothes that looked different from the other children at school. Ut and her sisters were wearing ao dai (ow▪zeye). Ao dai are high-necked, long sleeved dresses that are slit up to the waist and worn with long pants. Young children in grade school in Vietnam sometimes wear uniforms. Boys wear

long sleeved white shirts and dark blue pants. Girls wear white blouses and blue skirts.

- Why do you think Ut and her sisters wore what they did on the first day of school?
- What did Ut and her sisters wear to school the next day? Why?
- Have you ever been teased about what you were wearing? How did you feel? How do you think Ut felt when Raymond teased her?
- What do you like to wear to school?
- Do you think everyone should dress the same way?
- If you visited a school in Vietnam, do you think the children would be dressed like you?

Extend Your Experience

Partner Stories

- paper
- pencils

Point out to students that Raymond wrote a biography about Ut. In doing so, he learned many things about her and began to understand who she was. He discovered that while she had a very different background from him, she also had some similar feelings and emotions. Group children in pairs and invite them to take turns telling their partners about themselves. Older students can write down the information just as Raymond did for Ut. Younger students can share what they learned about their partners orally.

Vietnamese Fair

- *Look What We've Brought You from Vietnam* by Phyllis Shalant

Raymond, Ut, and their classmates organized a Vietnamese fair to raise money for Ut's mother to come to the United States. The children experienced many new sights, sounds, and tastes as they enjoyed eating rice cakes and sesame cookies, making a rainbow dragon, and greeting each other by saying, "Chao buoi sang." Plan a Vietnamese fair with your students to promote cultural awareness and to give your students a taste of Ut's world. Use *Look What We've Brought You from Vietnam* by Phyllis Shalant (see the bibliography on page 207) for some great planning ideas. The book provides directions for making dragon puppets and kites, recipes for making rice soup and moon cakes, and instructions for playing several Vietnamese games.

Rice Noodles

- rice sticks
- pan
- boiling water

Little Quang was playing with rice noodles and stringing them from cup hooks while Ut and her father were preparing dinner. Rice noodles are long thin noodles made from rice. They are also called "rice sticks." Vietnamese add rice sticks to chicken broth along with chicken, chopped green onions, shredded cabbage, and spices. The rice sticks can also be stir-fried with meat, vegetables, mushrooms, and soy sauce. You can buy rice sticks at any Asian food store. Make some rice sticks to enjoy with your students according to the directions on the package. Ask students to compare the taste and texture of rice sticks with other types of noodles they have eaten.

Learning and Literature

- *Toad Is the Uncle of Heaven* by Jeanne M. Lee

Ut was very unsure about going to her new American school on the very first day. Point out to children some of the differences Ut noticed about her new school (children raising their hands and speaking individually rather than chanting their lessons in unison, plus a new language). Education is highly valued in Vietnam and teachers are considered some of the most important members of society. Vietnamese children are unfamiliar with hands-on activities and cooperative learning groups which are so common in the United States. Although educational methods may differ, help students realize that there are many ways school children all over the world are the same. They have some of the same feelings, needs, likes, and dislikes.

Children in schools all over the world enjoy listening to their teacher read stories. Read the Vietnamese folk tale *Toad Is the Uncle of Heaven* by Jeanne M. Lee (see the bibliography on page 207) to the students. After enjoying the story, ask children if they have ever heard a story that has a similar plot. Children may make comparisons between the journey Toad, the Bees, Rooster, and Tiger made to see the King of Heaven to the journey Dorothy and her friends made to see the Wizard of Oz.

The Eye of the Needle

Retold and illustrated by Teri Sloat
New York: Dutton Children's Books, 1990

Synopsis

Amik, a young Yupik boy, is sent out by his grandmother to find food. With hunger overpowering him, Amik eats everything he catches, which includes a series of animals of ever-increasing size. When he returns to his grandmother empty-handed, he is surprised to learn that he actually brought back more than he realized.

Background

Eskimos are the native inhabitants of the arctic and subarctic areas of North America. The name "Eskimo" was given to them by the Algonquin Indians. The word means "people who eat their food raw." Eskimos call themselves "Inuit." This word means "the people." There are two forms of the Inuit language—"Yupik" is spoken by the Inuit who live in the southern part of Alaska and "Inupik" is spoken by the Inuit who live in northern Alaska, Canada, and Greenland. The authors of this story have lived and taught in Yupik villages and are eager to preserve the Yupik culture by retelling its authentic stories.

Deepen Your Understanding

1. Modern Inuit buy most of their clothing, but traditionally they have used animal skins to make hooded jackets called "parkas"

and boots called "mukluks." Amik's grandmother used an ivory needle to mend Amik's parka. Years ago, ivory was used to make many tools because it was readily available from the tusks of walrus.

- Have you ever tried to make or mend clothes? What kinds of tools did you use?
- What type of fabric would you use to make a jacket?
- Why do you think the Inuit used animal skins to make their clothes?

2. A sod house, as depicted in the story, was made of soil and built partly underground. Building the house partially underground helped to keep out the cold winds. Invite students to compare Amik's home with homes they have seen?

- How is Amik's home like homes you have seen before? How is it different?
- How do you keep your home warm inside during cold weather? How did Amik and his grandmother keep their home warm?
- What is your home made of? What was Amik's home made of?
- Would you like to live in Amik's house? Do you think he would like to live in your home? Why or why not?

3. Amik and his grandmother looked for specific signs that told them spring was near. They waited for the sun to melt the ice and for the spring breeze. Help students understand that warmer weather in polar regions is very limited. Cold is a constant companion. Except for three months of the year, the land remains frozen. Encourage students to think about the signs that tell them that spring is near where they live.

- How do you know when it is spring where you live?
- What is your favorite part of spring?
- Why do you think Amik and his grandmother were glad spring had come?
- Is the weather more often cold or warm where you live? Which type of weather do you like best? Why?
- Would you like to live where Amik lives?

4. Amik was excited that his grandmother finally thought he was big enough to go out and hunt for food. Encourage students to compare Amik's job with responsibilities they have at home. Invite children to consider tasks they hope to be able to do as they get older.

- How do you think Amik felt when his grandmother told him he could go out and hunt for food?
- What jobs do you do to help your family?
- If you were going to get food for your family, where would you go?

- Why do you think Amik did not go to a store to get food?
- What jobs do you hope to be able to do when you get older that you can't do now?

Extend Your Experience

Sea Creature Mobiles

- construction paper
- scissors
- crayons or markers
- hole punch
- thread
- wire coat hangers

Alaska is a land of many kinds of fish and sea mammals. Most of these creatures are included in the diet. Although Amik used his bare hands to land his catches, the Inuit often hunt whales, seals, and walruses with harpoons. Invite students to recall the names of the fish and mammals Amik ate and to place them in order according to size (needlefish, hooligan, salmon, seal, walrus, whale).

Then divide the class into cooperative groups of six. Each student in a group can draw one of Amik's "snacks." Have students cooperatively decide who will draw which fish or mammal so that all six are drawn. Encourage children to work together so that the fish and mammals are drawn according to scale—the needlefish being the smallest and the whale being the largest. Invite students to cut their drawings out and punch a small hole at the top of each one. Using thread, suspend each sea creature from a wire coat hanger to create a mobile.

Yupik Tales

As in many cultures, the Yupik have a strong oral storytelling tradition. Storytellers were important people. In a land where families might have to stay in their homes for days at a time because of bad weather, storytelling became an art. Invite students to practice retelling the story The Eye of the Needle to one another. Encourage students to distinguish real from make-believe. Then invite students to create their own tales and share them with the class in an oral storytelling session.

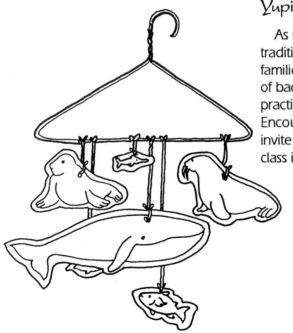

Smoke Hole

- glass jar
- small candle
- clay
- matches

In the winter, the Yupik spent most of their time inside their huts. They used an open fire for heat and cooking. The huts were built with an opening in the roof called a "smoke hole" to provide an outlet for the smoke generated from the fire. An open tunnel entrance to the hut provided air intake for the fire. Demonstrate the importance of these features in the Yupik home by carefully presenting the following experiment.

Place a candle in a small clay base so it stands upright. Light the candle and cover it with the glass jar. The candle will extinguish itself when the oxygen inside the glass jar is consumed. However, the smoke will remain inside the jar. Explain to students that this is what would happen if the Yupik huts were not made with smoke holes. Invite the students to look again at the pictures of the huts in the story. Ask students if they have a fireplace in their homes. If so, ask them to explain what keeps the smoke from filling their homes.

Ajegaung

- unsharpened pencils
- yarn or string
- heavy cardboard
- scissors
- crayons or markers
- tape

Amik was very skillful in his ability to make many fine catches as he searched for food. Give your students an opportunity to try their skill at making some good "catches" by playing an Inuit game called "ajegaung." It is a holes-and-pin game played by tossing an object with holes into the air and catching it by one of its holes on a pin.

Prepare a piece of heavy cardboard for each student by cutting it into a fish shape and making several holes in the "fish." The fish should be about the size of your hand. The holes should be large enough for an unsharpened pencil (pin) to fit through easily. Invite children to decorate their fish shapes using crayons or markers. Help students tie one end of a piece of yarn or string through one of the holes in the fish and tie the other end to an unsharpened pencil. Use tape to secure the string to the pencil. Invite students to hold the "pin" in one hand with the eraser down. Show the children how to toss the fish into the air and then catch the fish using the pencil to pass through one of the holes.

DIVERSITY
Around the
WORLD

Galimoto

Written by Karen Lynn Williams and illustrated by Catherine Stock
New York: Lothrop, Lee & Shepard Books, 1990

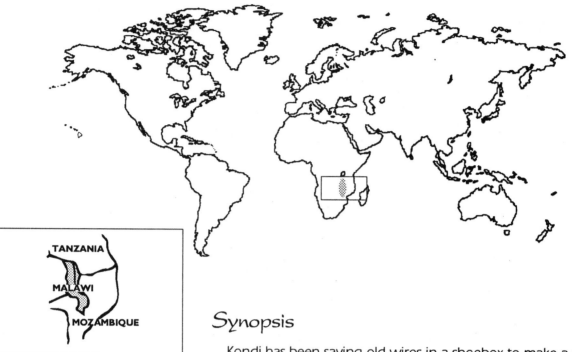

Synopsis

Kondi has been saving old wires in a shoebox to make a special toy called a "galimoto." When he realizes he does not have enough supplies, Kondi finds clever and resourceful ways of gathering the extra materials that he needs. By the end of the day, Kondi is proudly pushing his pickup, fashioned from wire, over the dusty path of the Malawi village.

Background

Malawi is a long, narrow country in southeast Africa that is primarily rural as depicted in the story. Karen Lynn Williams lived in Malawi for several years and was intrigued by the village children. She was impressed with their skill at creating a popular toy they called a "galimoto."

Deepen Your Understanding

1. Notice the clothing worn by the Malawian villagers as illustrated in *Galimoto*. Malawian women wear skirts and dresses made from brightly colored and patterned cloth that they wrap around their bodies. Their skirts are always long enough to cover their knees and they never wear shorts or pants. Men in Malawi wear Western-style shirts and pants and often wear shorts. Point out

the clothing that Kondi and those in his village are wearing. Encourage children to compare and contrast this clothing with their own.

- Describe the clothing the villagers in the story are wearing. How is it the same or different from your clothing?
- Malawians enjoy wearing clothes made from bright colors and beautiful patterns. Describe the colors and patterns from some of your clothes. What color or pattern is your favorite? Why?
- What do the Malawian villagers wear on their feet?
- Do you like to go barefoot? What kind of weather is best for going barefoot?
- What do you think the weather is like in Malawi?

2. About ninety percent of Malawians live in rural villages in thatched huts. These small villages are called "mudzi." The huts' walls are made by covering a pole frame with mud. The roofs are made of straw or woven leaves. Many villages are often surrounded by fences called "bomas" to prevent lions or leopards from entering. Invite children to notice the huts in the pictures and to find the fence surrounding the huts in one of the illustrations. Help children understand that people around the world often build their homes from materials that are readily available and that are appropriate for the weather conditions of the area.

- What does it look like the homes in Malawi are made from?
- What is your home made from?
- Why do you think people around the world make homes from different materials?
- If you were going to build a house, what would you make it out of? Why?

3. Although Kondi lives in a place that may be very different from where your students live, he, like many children, enjoys collecting and saving special things. Ask children to recall some of the special things Kondi saved in his shoebox. Encourage children to predict what Kondi might do with some of his special things. Then invite children to imagine what they might save in a special box.

- What kinds of things did Kondi save in his special shoebox?
- What do you think he will do with the ball of plastic bags tied with string?
- Kondi made a galimoto from the wire he collected. What else could you make using wires?
- If Kondi had come to your home looking for more wire, how would you have helped him?
- If you had a special box, what would you keep in it?
- Have you ever made something from materials you have gathered? What?

4. Point out some of Kondi's personality characteristics based on his actions. For example, Ufulu laughed at his brother's idea of

making a galimoto, but Kondi remained "confident." Kondi didn't have enough wire to make his pickup, but he was "resourceful" in finding ways to get more materials. Kondi's uncle said he had no wire, but Kondi's "clever" thinking paid off. Encourage children to think about Kondi's personality based on his actions and to compare and contrast their own characteristics with Kondi's.

- How would you describe Kondi by the way he acted?
- Has anyone ever laughed at one of your ideas? How did you feel? What did you do?
- What is the first thing you do when you can't find what you are looking for?
- Why do you think Kondi's uncle thought he was a clever boy? Do you agree? What does it mean to be clever? Do you think you are clever? Why or why not?

Extend Your Experience

Making Corn Cakes

Maize (or corn) is the staple food in Malawi and most meals include some kind of corn dish. The corn is often pounded and crushed into flour. Point out the grinding mill in the story and Kondi's mother and sister pounding the maize. The cornmeal is often mixed with water to make a cornmeal porridge called "nsima" or it is baked into flat corn cakes. Ask students what kinds of foods they have eaten that are made from corn (corn chips, corn tortillas, corn bread, corn dogs, cereal, and so on). Make corn cakes with your students.

Corn Cakes	
• ¼ cup (60 ml) cornmeal	Combine the cornmeal and water in a
• 1 cup (250 ml) water	small saucepan and stir over medium
• 3 Tbsp (45 ml) butter	heat until thick. Add butter and stir.
• ¾ cup (200 ml) flour	Set aside to cool. Combine flour,
• ½ tsp (2.5 ml) salt	salt, baking powder, and baking soda
• ½ tsp (2.5 ml) baking powder	in a bowl. Stir eggs, milk, and sour
• ¼ tsp (1.25 ml) baking soda	cream into the cooled cornmeal
• 2 eggs (lightly beaten)	mixture. Gently fold in the flour
• ½ cup (125 ml) milk	mixture. Stir thoroughly. Drop batter
• ¼ cup (60 ml) sour cream	by tablespoons onto a hot, greased
	griddle. Cook until the edges of the
	corn cakes are dry and the tops are
	bubbling (about 1 minute). Flip and
	cook 1 minute on the other side.
	Enjoy!

Work Songs

Although many lifestyles are represented in various parts of Africa, a common denominator among Africans is music. Like many other cultures, Africans not only celebrate important events and ceremonies with music, but music is also a part of their daily lives. Sometimes, Africans enjoy creating words and melodies as they go about their daily chores. Remind students that in *Galimoto*, Kondi's mother and sister sang as they pounded the maize. Kondi's friends also used a song to call their friend to come and play. Ask children what songs they enjoy singing and when they usually sing them. Invite children to create work songs to accompany their classroom tasks or home chores and share their melodies with the class.

Free Time Fun

- pipe cleaners
- *Building Your Own Toys* by Sabine Lohf (optional)

Encourage students to notice what Kondi and the other village children like to do for fun. Invite children to compare their free time activities and toys with the activities and toys from Africa. Ask children what activities Kondi and his friends enjoyed that they have tried or would like to try.

Provide students with pipe cleaners, as well as other odds and ends from which to fashion their own galimoto. Suggest that students can create a type of vehicle, such as a car, truck, bicycle, train, or helicopter as Kondi did, if they wish. Remind students that a galimoto is a push toy and therefore needs one long piece of wire attached to the top so it can be pushed along the ground. As a result of this activity, children may be inspired to follow Kondi's example and collect more materials to make other toys. *Building Your Own Toys* by Sabine Lohf (see the bibliography on page 207) is an excellent resource of simple toys children can make from easily collected materials.

Balancing Baskets

- empty baskets or plastic containers

People in Malawi carry their loads in baskets on their heads as do many people around the world. It takes some practice and skill to feel comfortable and do this successfully. But once it is mastered, carrying loads on one's head is a very useful skill that eases the work load and frees the hands for other activities. Encourage children to try mastering this balancing skill by carrying some baskets or plastic containers on their heads as they walk around the room.

Rehema's Journey: A Visit in Tanzania

Written and photographed by Barbara A. Margolies
New York: Scholastic, 1990

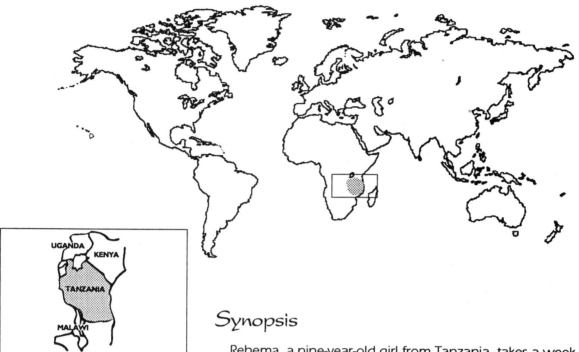

Synopsis

Rehema, a nine-year-old girl from Tanzania, takes a week-long trip with her father to visit the Ngorongoro Crater. Along the way, Rehema visits the big city of Arusha, passes by a Waarusha village, and stops to visit some Maasai friends.

Background

This beautifully written account of Rehema's journey with her father illustrates the diversity within Tanzania. Barbara Margolies has visited Tanzania many times and hopes that through her book, children all over the world will get a glimpse of life in this east African country.

Deepen Your Understanding

1. Rehema's new house was made of cement. Her old house was made of mud and cow dung. The houses outside Arusha looked very different from Rehema's house. They were round houses with thatched roofs. The Maasai houses were made of sticks and grass and covered with cow dung. Help students understand that the homes people live in depend on the region in which they live and their lifestyles. Compare the diversity of homes in Tanzania with homes in North America.

- What did Rehema notice was different about the houses she saw on her trip compared to her own house?
- How are the homes in this story different from your home? How are they the same?
- Why do you think homes have different shapes and are made with different materials?
- How would you describe your home? What is it made of?

2. Rehema was both excited and a little scared as she began her first trip away from home. She had never been to a big city before and she had never been away from her mother for a whole week. Invite children to compare a first-time experience they have had with Rehema's.

- Why do you think Rehema felt a little scared to go on her week-long trip?
- Have you ever gone on a trip away from home? Were you scared? Why? Why not?
- Have you ever been afraid to try something for the first time? When?
- Why do you think "first times" are so scary?

3. Rehema and her father visited their Maasai friends. The Maasai are a group of people who lived very near Rehema and yet spoke a different language and lived very different lives. Help children recognize that Rehema and her father had a friendship with people who lived differently than they did.

- Have you ever met someone who spoke a different language than you do?
- Have you ever met someone who dressed very differently than you do? What did you think about these people?
- Would you like to meet Rehema or some of her Maasai friends?
- What one question would you like to ask Rehema and her friends if you had a chance to visit Tanzania?
- What one thing would you like to tell them about yourself?

4. Rehema and her father stopped at the market in Arusha before continuing their journey. Rehema saw piles of salt, a bundle of miswaki, and fresh pineapples and mangoes. In a typical market, everything is displayed in neat stacks or straight lines. Vendors arrange spices, such as salt, into cone-like piles. Spices are usually sold by the scoopful and placed into small pieces of newspaper or into the shopper's own container. The entire market is bright, filled with a brilliant array of colors, and wonderfully organized.

- How is the market Rehema visited different from the market you usually go to? How is it the same?
- How are spices sold at the market you visit?
- If you could visit the market in Tanzania, what would you like to buy? Why?

Extend Your Experience

ABC's of Gardening

- clay or plastic pots, 6" to 8" (15.3 cm to 20.4 cm) in diameter
- soil
- herb seeds

Tanzanians work predominantly in agriculture and a majority of them live in rural areas. In school, children not only learn to read and write, but they also learn how to plant and care for tea and coffee bushes, vegetables, fruits, and flowers. Coffee and tea are Tanzania's largest export crops. Give your students an opportunity to learn about and care for a small herb garden. Invite students to plant herb seeds in pots. Most herbs demand full sunshine and are best grown sitting in a sunny window. Basil, chives, dill, fennel, parsley, rosemary, sage, mint, marjoram, and tarragon are suggested. Basil is very hardy and you should have little difficulty growing it. When placed in full sun, the seeds should sprout in about a week. The seedlings then rapidly develop into mature plants.

African Animals

- *Wild Animals of Africa ABC* by Hope Ryden (optional)

Ngorongoro Crater, a collapsed volcano, is home to millions of birds and hundreds of animals. It is the home of the largest permanent population of game animals in all of Africa. No other place on earth can a visitor see wildlife in such variety and abundance. *Wild Animals of Africa ABC* by Hope Ryden (see the bibliography on page 207) is an excellent source of beautiful photographs of African wildlife. The back of the book includes a brief description of each animal from A to Z, including the unique dik-diks, klipspringers, and meerkats. Show the pictures of each animal listed below from *Rehema's Journey* or *Wild Animals of Africa ABC* and invite children to learn the Swahili pronunciation.

English	Swahili
elephant	tembo (TEM■bow)
cheetah	duma (DOO■ma)
hippopotamus	kiboko (ki■BOW■kow)
lion	simba (SIM■bah)
ostrich	mbuni (mm■BOO■ni)
rhinoceros	kifaru (ki■FAH■roo)
zebra	punda milia (POON■dah mi■LIAH)

Journey by Bus

- 12" x 18" (30.6 cm x 45.9 cm) construction paper
- crayons or markers

Invite students to recall the interesting sights Rehema saw on her bus journey to Ngorongoro Crater. For example, Rehema saw a boy taking care of the family cows, children carrying heavy loads on their heads, mothers washing clothes in a stream, and a boy paddling down a river on a tree-log boat. Then invite students to name all the things they might see if they rode a bus from their home to school, a nearby park, or a store. For example, your students might see traffic lights, billboards, and office buildings.

Invite children to draw a big bus in the center of a 12" x 18" (30.6 cm x 45.9 cm) piece of construction paper. Have children draw three things Rehema saw from her bus window across the top of the paper. Then have children draw three things they would see from their bus window across the bottom of the paper.

Until We Meet Again

- world map

Rehema said "kwaheri," which means goodbye in Swahili, when she left the animals at Ngorongoro. Baba said goodbye in Maasai, and Rehema knew it was time to leave when she heard the words "ole sere." Invite students to learn how to say goodbye in more than one language, just as Rehema was able to do. Point out on the world map where each greeting is commonly used.

French—au revoir (oh■ruh■VWAHR)
German—auf Wiedersehen (owf■VEE■der■zay■en)
Hawaiian—aloha (uh■LOH■ha)
Italian—ciao (chow)
Japanese—(sigh■uh■NAR■uh)
Korean—(awn■nyung■HEE■gah■say■yo)
Spanish—adios (AH■dee■ohs)
Vietnamese—(chow■nee■yeh)

(For some languages, only the phonetic spelling is provided.)

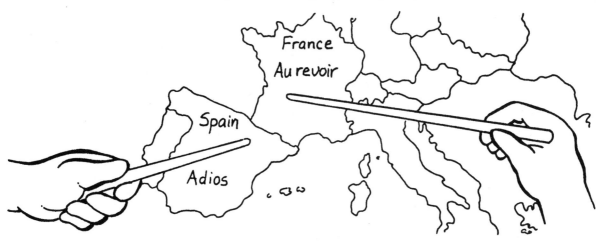

The Village of Round and Square Houses

Written and illustrated by Ann Grifalconi
Boston: Little, Brown and Company, 1986

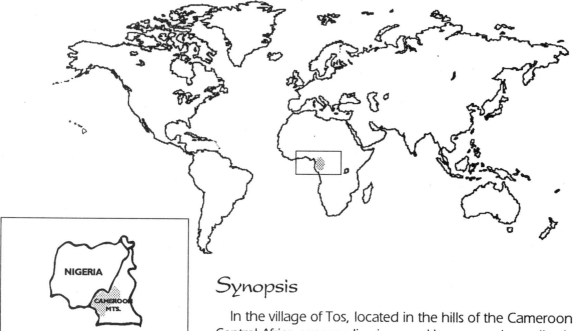

Synopsis

In the village of Tos, located in the hills of the Cameroons in Central Africa, women live in round houses and men live in square ones. A young girl who grew up in this remote village tells how this came to be.

Background

The remote village of Tos is located in Central Africa near the side of an almost extinct volcano known as Naka Mountain. Ann Grifalconi has had a long-standing interest in African cultures. She wrote this story after visiting the village of Tos. Her beautiful illustrations earned her a Caldecott Honor Award in 1986.

Deepen Your Understanding

1. In Western cultures, formal book knowledge is the criteria used to measure wisdom. In Tos, worth is measured by the knowledge of history and traditions, survival abilities, and the accumulated wisdom that comes only with age. Respect for age is therefore important because wisdom comes with experience. As depicted in the story, it was proper and respectful to put out the low, wooden stool for Gran'pa Oma and to unroll the grass mat for Uncle Domo. Gran'pa ate first because he was the oldest.

- Do you think older people should be treated specially? Why or why not?
- Do the oldest people in your family receive special treatment? What?
- If you ate according to age, who would eat first in your family? Who would eat last?

2. In the village of Tos, everyone in the family did not live in the same house. The women lived in round houses and the men lived in square houses. They lived together peacefully because each one had "a place to be apart, and a time to be together."

   - Does everyone in your family live in the same place?
   - When do you like to be apart from other people in your family?
   - Where do you go to be alone?
   - When do you most enjoy being together with your family?

3. Review some of the customs associated with mealtime in the village of Tos. In the story, each person had a job to do. Diners would sit on the floor and wash with a bowl of heated water and towels before and after eating. Everyone would eat in turn from a large bowl and dip the food with three fingers rather than use utensils.

   - If someone from the village visited your home, what is the first thing they might find different about mealtime in your home?
   - What are some ways mealtime is the same in the village of Tos as it is in your home?
   - How do you help prepare a meal?
   - If you could visit this village in Africa, what would you like best about mealtime there?
   - How often do your grandparents eat dinner with you?

4. When Gran'pa Oma and Uncle Domo asked to see the children, they would ask each one what he or she had learned that day. Elders challenge younger members not to be content with merely knowing "how" but in searching for "why." They know that "how" is easily learned but "why" takes a lifetime of learning.

   - When asked what they learned that day, what do you think the children might have answered?
   - What would you answer if someone asked you what you had learned today?
   - Do you think the children in this African village learn the same things you do? Why or why not?
   - Have you ever wondered "why" something is the way it is or "why" something happened as it did? What? Do you know the answer to your "why" question? How could you find out?

Extend Your Experience

African Storytelling

Gran'ma Tika was the best storyteller in the whole village. Ask children why they think this was so. They might suggest that it was because she had interesting things to tell or that she spoke dramatically using descriptive words and an expressive voice. Invite children to work in pairs, each telling a story to the other. After some practice and refinement, ask volunteers to share their tales with the class.

Round and Square Houses

- magazines
- construction paper
- glue
- scissors

It seemed natural to the little girl in the story that men live in square houses and women live in round ones. She thought everyone in the world lived that way until she left the village. Brainstorm about the different kinds and shapes of homes in which people live. Encourage students to describe the shape of their house or apartment. Invite students to cut pictures from magazines of different dwellings and make a home collage to display in the room. Children might also enjoy hearing the story *Who's in Rabbit's House* by Verna Aardema (see the bibliography on page 206).

Fou-Fou

- ingredients and utensils to prepare tapioca pudding

Fou-fou is a dish served in many African countries. In the village of Tos it is made from white cassava root. The cassava roots are peeled and left to soak for several days. After cutting out the hard cores, they are placed in a pan of water which is brought to a boil and then allowed to simmer for about ten minutes. The softened cassavas are then pounded until they form a soft dough. The large white grains, known as tapioca, come from the cassava root. Prepare tapioca pudding without using sugar as a fou-fou variation for your students to sample. Encourage students to use the three-finger method to eat the pudding rather than using a spoon.

Making Groundnut Stew

"Groundnuts" is the term used in Africa for peanuts, since these nuts grow under the ground. Provide students with some peanuts in the shell to count, crack, and eat. Discuss how the peanuts grow and are harvested. Because West Africa is a main area for peanut cultivation, groundnut stew is eaten by many families. The stew usually consists of peanuts and some type of fish or meat. Invite some parent volunteers to help out as you prepare and share this African dish with your students. Be aware of any student allergies to peanuts.

Groundnut Stew	
• 2 lbs (900 g) beef stew meat	Brown the stew meat in oil. Add
• 1 cup (250 ml) chopped onion	the onion. Gradually mix in the
• 1 cup (250 ml) peanut butter	peanut butter, curry powder, and
• 3 Tbsp (45 ml) curry powder	flour. Add beef stock, celery,
• 3 Tbsp (45 ml) flour	carrots, squash, and peanuts.
• 2 cans beef stock	Simmer until the vegetables are
• 1/2 cup (125 ml) chopped celery	tender. Prepare a bowl of heated
• 4 carrots (chopped)	water and provide towels for
• 2 squash (sliced)	students to wash their hands
• 2 cups roasted peanuts	before and after eating.
• bowl of heated water and towels	

When Africa Was Home

Written by Karen Lynn Williams and illustrated by Floyd Cooper
New York: Orchard Books, 1991

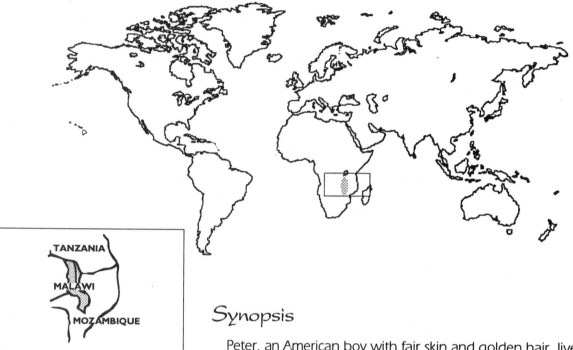

Synopsis

Peter, an American boy with fair skin and golden hair, lived his early years in Africa. He became one with the children who called him "achimwene," which means "little brother" in Chichewa. Even though his family spoke of life in the United States, he did not want to leave Africa. After moving to America, his greatest desire was to return to the place he called home.

Background

"Home" for Peter was Malawi (mah•LAH•wee), a land of great scenic beauty in southeastern Africa. Most of its inhabitants live in small, rural villages of a few hundred people. Karen Lynn Williams and her family spent three and a half years in Africa while serving in the Peace Corps.

Deepen Your Understanding

1. Chichewa is the national language of Malawi, although school children are required to learn English as well. Review some of the Chichewa words used in the story. Compare appropriate African greetings and behaviors with those common in America.

   - What did Peter call his nanny? What special names do you use for your mother, father, baby-sitter, or grandparents?

- Peter and Yekha asked each other how they slept when they greeted each other. What do you usually say when you see your friends?
- Peter thought people "talked funny" in America. Why do you think he felt that way?
- Did you ever think that someone may think your words sound "funny"?
- Have you ever heard someone speak in another language? What did you think when you first heard the unfamiliar words?

2. Although Peter was not African, he still considered Africa his kwatu (home). Stimulate students to think about what makes a place feel like home. For Peter, home was where his surroundings were most comfortable and familiar to him.

- Why do you think Peter would rather live in Africa than America?
- If Peter stayed in America longer, do you think he would start to call it his home? Why or why not?
- If you were asked to move to Africa, do you think you could call it your new home?
- If you had been Peter, would you rather live in America or Africa? Why?

3. The region of Africa in which Peter lived is one of Africa's most scenic rural countries. The many beautiful sights include wild animals, such as a rare species of antelope called "nyala" found only in Malawi. Point out some unique features of Africa as depicted in the story (beautiful moonlit sky, sparkling stars, ant-hills, paw-paw trees, maize fields, sugar cane). Compare and contrast this environment with the ones in which your students live.

- What are some things Peter saw in Africa that you have never seen?
- What are some things you have seen that Peter would probably not see in Africa?
- Peter climbed a paw-paw tree and sat in the shade of a jacaranda tree. What are some names of trees in your neighborhood?
- If you had a chance to go to Africa, what would you most like to see?
- If someone from Africa visited you, what would you most like to show them?

4. Peter was accepted by his African neighbors, even though his fair skin and golden hair made him look very different. When Peter went to America, it was his turn to be accepting of differences he would find there. Help children understand that diversity among people should be met with understanding and an open mind.

- Have you ever felt like you looked or acted very differently from the people around you? What made you feel that way?
- What do you do when you meet someone who "talks funny" or looks different than you do?
- Do you think people should all try to look and act the same way? Why or why not?

Extend Your Experience

Sound Sort

- chalk or 3" x 5" (7.6 cm x 12.7 cm) cards

Just as Peter saw many sights in Africa that he would not see in America, so there were also many wonderful African sounds he became accustomed to hearing. Using chalk, draw outlines of Africa and America on the pavement outside and print the name of the appropriate country inside each outline. Then, one by one, name the sounds listed here. Ask children to stand inside the outline of the place where the sound would most likely be heard.

Or, as an alternative to this activity, give each student a 3" x 5" (7.6 cm x 12.7 cm) card with the word "Africa" printed on it and another card with the word "America" printed on it. Ask students to hold up the appropriate card as the sounds are named.

vacuum cleaner
hippo mooing
hyena groaning
drums beating
ice clinking in a glass
snow crunching

Challenge students to suggest other sounds to add to the list.

Another Point of View

Because Peter lived in Africa, he viewed American culture as being very strange. He thought a vacuum cleaner looked like a long snake. He described a television as a box with talking people inside. Invite students to see their own culture from another point of view. Encourage children to describe items that are very familiar to them in a way that a person who was seeing them for the first time might describe them. Remind students of Peter's observations when he first came to America. Challenge students to creatively describe a lawn sprinkler, a refrigerator, a computer, and so on.

African Designs

- clay
- plastic knife
- empty spools
- cookie cutters
- vegetables, such as potatoes and carrots
- tempera paint
- crayons and markers
- construction paper
- cardboard
- scissors

The yellow and blue designs on Peter's ski cap reminded him of his home in Africa. Many beautiful designs and patterns can be found there everywhere. Baskets are woven and beautifully decorated. Food containers and trays are carved. Cloth is woven in patterns and dyed to create interesting designs. Sometimes even the walls of mud houses are used like an artist's canvas. Invite children to create some interesting designs and patterns using a variety of materials.

Students can create carved designs in a piece of clay using a pencil tip or the edge of a plastic knife. Children can create interesting stamped designs by dipping empty spools, cookie cutters, or vegetable shapes in tempera paint and then stamping them on a sheet of paper. Or, students can use a stencil shape cut from cardboard to make a repetitive design. Display the variety of patterns around the room. Ask students what each reminds them of as they consider why Peter's hat might have reminded him so much of his home in Africa.

Singing Drums

- variety of containers and boxes

As Peter went to sleep each night in Africa, he could hear the drums singing in the distance. Drums are an important instrument in Africa and there are many different kinds. African drums speak, tell stories, and as Peter noticed, the drums can sing. Invite children to create different sounds and rhythms by beating a variety of overturned containers and boxes. Encourage students to make loud sounds, soft sounds, and slow and quick sounds as they create a "singing" story.

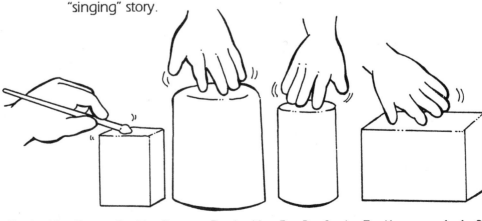

Tiddalick the Frog

Written by Susan Nunes and illustrated by Ju-Hong Chen
New York: Atheneum, 1989

Synopsis

Long ago in the Dreamtime, there lived a gigantic frog named Tiddalick. His powerful voice sounded like thunder and his hops shook the ground for miles. To quench his enormous thirst, he drank the riverbed dry. His enormous stomach now held all the fresh water of the world. As the land soon showed signs of a serious drought, the other animals planned how they might convince Tiddalick to release his "precious load" and restore life to the earth once again.

Background

Australia, the world's biggest island and smallest continent, is called "down under" because it lies entirely south of the equator. The Aborigines were the first known people to live on this small continent. According to Aboriginal beliefs, the world was created by spirits in a period of the distant past called the "Dreamtime." In this Dreamtime, spirits that took the form of people and animals appeared. These beings created everything in the world and then sank back into the earth.

Deepen Your Understanding

1. The characters' actions in the story illustrate aspects of their personalities. For example, Tiddalick proved his stubbornness and insensitivity by simply rolling his eyes when the animals told him their troubles. Wombat showed his wisdom by thinking of a plan to solve the problem. Encourage students to see other personality traits among the characters and to compare the characters with themselves.

   - In what ways are you like Tiddalick? How are you different?
   - Have you ever thought of an idea that no one else has thought of like Wombat did? How did it make you feel?
   - How would you describe Noyang the eel?
   - Which character in the story do you think you are most like? Why?

2. It was common knowledge, even for the animals, that you can't keep water in your mouth while you laugh. So, the animals tried many ways to get the frog to laugh. Encourage students to consider the importance of humor in our lives and to discuss what makes them laugh and smile.

   - Which animal in the story would have made you laugh? Why?
   - What is the funniest thing you have ever seen or heard?
   - What would you do to try to make a friend of yours laugh or smile?
   - What usually makes you laugh?
   - Being thirsty put Tiddalick in a very "ill humor." What puts you in an "ill humor"?

3. The Aborigines have passed on from generation to generation their beliefs about the creation of their land in the Dreamtime through storytelling, song, and dance. Invite students to distinguish real from make-believe in the folktale about Tiddalick.

   - Which parts of the story do you think are real?
   - Which parts do you think are make-believe? Why?
   - What do you think would have happened to the animals if they had not succeeded in getting Tiddalick to release the water?
   - What is a drought?
   - What are the animals doing to make sure there is not another drought?
   - What can you do to help prevent a drought where you live?

4. Living things need water to survive, which is why all the animals in the story agreed that they were "doomed" as they sat beside the dry riverbed. A human being needs about 2 1/2 quarts (2.4 l) of water a day to stay healthy. This can come from drinking water or other beverages and from water contained in the foods we eat.

- How much water do you think you need to live each day?
- Have you ever felt really thirsty?
- How long do you think you could go without water?
- Do you think people in all parts of the world have the same amount of water to drink? Why or why not?

Extend Your Experience

Australian Animals

- tagboard
- marker

Tiddalick was gigantic. He was so big that his shadow turned day into night. He was so powerful that his voice drowned the thunder and he was so heavy that a single hop shook the ground for miles and miles. Although Tiddalick is a folktale character, there are many amazing animals in Australia. Describe each Australian animal mentioned in the story briefly and write each name on the chalkboard. Review what each animal looks like using the pictures in *Tiddalick the Frog*.

Making Lamingtons

The animals were undoubtedly excited and relieved when Tiddalick allowed the water to gush from his mouth and again fill the earth. A celebration of such an event might include a dessert called "Lamingtons"—a favorite of Australian children.

Lamingtons	
• yellow cake mix	Bake the cake in a 9" x 13" (22.9 cm x
• 3 cups (750 ml) powdered sugar	33.1 cm) pan as directed on the package. Cool and cut the cake into
• 1/3 cup (90 ml) cocoa	small squares. Sift powdered sugar
• 3 Tbsp (45 ml) melted butter	and cocoa together. Add melted butter and boiling water. Mix well.
• 1/2 cup (125 ml) boiling water	Place the bowl of icing in a saucepan about 1/4 full of simmering water. Using
• 3 cups (750 ml) shredded coconut	two forks, dip each square of cake into the hot icing and then roll the cake
	squares in coconut. Cover the cake
	squares on all six sides. Let the icing
	harden and enjoy!

Drought Danger

- gallon, quart, pint, and cup containers (or liter container with milliliters)

Australia is the driest continent and droughts there are common. In some places it does not rain for years. "Billabong" is an aboriginal word that means "dead river." It is usually used to describe a river or waterhole that contains water for only part of the year. This folktale about Tiddalick illustrates the need for water and the unfortunate circumstances resulting from drought conditions. Help students become aware of how much water they actually use each day and to consider ways they can conserve it.

Water-Holding Frog Cup

- 8" x 8" (20.4 cm x 20.4 cm) paper
- crayons or markers

There are about 180 species of frogs in Australia. One species of frog is called the "water-holding frog." Make frog drinking cups as a reminder of the many types of frogs in Australia and the need for all living things to have a bountiful supply of water.

Give each student an 8" square of paper. Have students fold the square in half diagonally. Bring point C to the center of line A-B. Turn the paper over and fold point A to point D. Fold top sheet of point B downward. Turn the cup over and repeat. Invite students to draw a frog on one side of their cup using crayons or markers. Encourage students to fill their water-holding frogs will water and enjoy a cool drink.

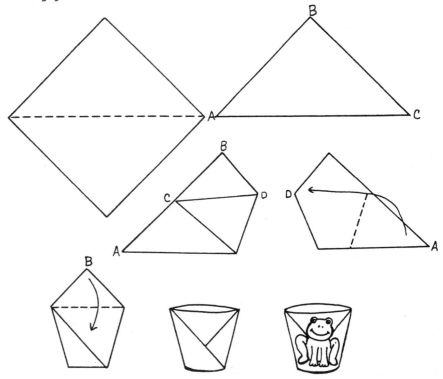

Ayu and the Perfect Moon

Written and illustrated by David Cox
London: The Bodley Head, 1984

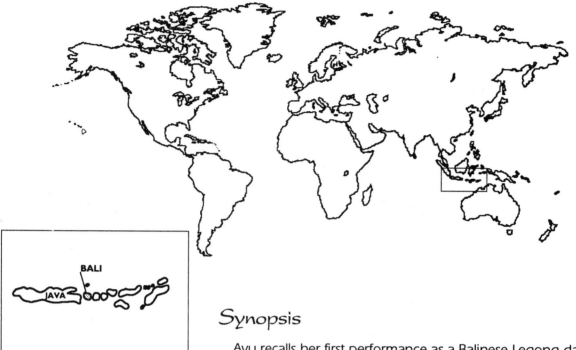

Synopsis

Ayu recalls her first performance as a Balinese Legong dancer as she describes her experience to three wide-eyed young girls. On the night of the full moon, Ayu, dressed in her beautiful red and gold dancer's costume, performs the dance of the angry bird to the smooth melody of the gamelan.

Background

Bali is an Indonesian island located just east of Java. The Balinese are famous for their skills in the arts. They have developed a rich tradition of music, dance, and theater. In fact, no celebration or holiday is complete without a special performance. David Cox traveled to Bali and met a young Legong dancer about whom this story is based.

Deepen Your Understanding

1. Ayu first performed the traditional Legong dance under the light of a full moon. She looked at the moon and watched it grow larger every night until the time was right for her performance. Timing is important to the Balinese. Traditionally, the Balinese consider the timing of a particular event as important as the event

itself. Encourage children to be "moon watchers" over the course of the next month and to observe how the changes in the moon signal the passage of time. Discuss other measures of time as well.

- Ayu knew it was the right time to perform by looking at the moon. How do you decide when it is the right time to do something?
- Why do you think Ayu was asked to perform on a night when the moon was full?
- What are some ways you keep track of time?

2. Balinese dancers often begin their dance training between the ages of 6 and 8. Since the dances often demand quick, rhythmic movements, they are often performed by children. While the Legong dance is performed by girls, boys have special dance parts as well.

- Do you think Ayu enjoyed performing? Why or why not?
- How do you think Ayu felt as she was putting on her costume and preparing for her big moment?
- How do you usually feel before you do something for the very first time?
- Do you like to dance? What kinds of dances do you like to do? Would you like to be a Balinese dancer? Why or why not?

3. Nearly every Balinese dance requires a special costume. The costumes are often very brilliant and rich looking. Sometimes elaborate masks are worn as well. Ayu wore a red and gold brocade dress and a beautiful, golden crown. Encourage children to describe Ayu's costume and to compare it with costumes they have seen or worn.

- Have you ever seen a performer who was wearing a costume? What did the costume look like?
- Why do you think dancers wear costumes?
- Have you ever worn a costume? When?
- If you had a chance to perform, what would you like to do and what would your costume look like?

4. Review the pictures in the book, looking closely at the people, houses, landscape, and animal and plant life. The illustrations depict a man herding his ducks, coconut and banana trees, and a man plowing his rice field. Encourage students to discuss the weather, climate, and life on this island.

- What types of jobs do people on the island of Bali do?
- Are these jobs the same or different from the jobs your neighbors do? Why?
- Name something Ayu saw in Bali that you have never seen where you live.
- Does any part of Bali remind you of a place you have visited? Where?

Extend Your Experience

Dancer's Crown

- 9" x 12" (22.9 cm x 30.6 cm) yellow construction paper
- white tissue paper
- glitter glue
- tape
- green pipe cleaners
- stapler
- X-acto knife (teacher use only)

Ayu wore a golden crown decorated with flowers from the frangipani tree. The frangipani is one of the best-known flowering trees in Indonesia. Though the tree is fairly small, the blossoms are quite large. Invite students to make a crown similar to the crown Ayu wore using construction paper, tissue paper flowers, and glitter glue.

Before beginning the project, use an X-acto knife to cut a wavy slit lengthwise across a 9" x 12" (22.9 cm x 30.6 cm) sheet of yellow construction paper for each student. Begin one inch from each side edge and two inches down from the top. Reinforce the ends of the paper with tape to prevent the slit from tearing into the one-inch margin on each side. The two-inch strip of the crown goes around the forehead, while the taller section stands erect behind the head.

Invite students to add glitter decorations to the crown. Help children make flowers by accordion-folding the length of an 8" x 4" (20.4 cm x 10.2 cm) piece of white tissue paper. Show the children how to fold a 6" (15.3 cm) green pipe cleaner over the center and twist to hold and form a stem. Open the tissue paper petals gently. Staple the flowers to the front of the crown. Hold a dance performance with your class and encourage the children to wear their dancer's crowns.

Gamelan Melody

- empty cartons and boxes
- cookie sheets or pie tins
- drinking glasses filled with water
- spoons
- xylophone (optional)

A "gamelan" (GAM•eh•lan) is an Indonesian orchestra consisting primarily of percussion instruments. Explain to the children that percussion instruments are those that are played by striking, shaking, or scraping. The basic instruments of the gamelan are drums, metal and wooden bars played much like a xylophone, and gongs.

Invite students to create some percussion instruments. For example, students can tap spoons against a cookie sheet or pie tin to make a gonging sound. Or, children can create rhythmic drum beats by tapping on any empty cartons or boxes turned upside down. Invite students to tap a commercial xylophone, if available, or create their own by tapping on drinking glasses filled with various amounts of water. The gamelan has no conductor, nor do the players have sheet music to follow. Players listen to one another and try to match their speed to the speed of the drummers. Encourage students to play their instruments cooperatively in small groups to create a musical "story."

Speaking Without Words

Some children might think of dancing as moving their legs and feet. Yet, in the Legong dance, the movement of the hands tells much of the story. Each gesture has a definite meaning. The arms, fingers, head, eyes, and neck do most of the dancing and "talking." Dancers in Southeast Asia are highly skilled artists and perform each movement with perfection. For example, the seemingly simple gesture of forming a perfect circle with the thumb and forefinger and then snapping it open and closed takes much practice to satisfy an accomplished Balinese dancer. Discuss other forms of dance that tell a story without words (ballet, Hawaiian dancing). Then invite children to create some hand movements and perform while other classmates play their gamelan instruments. Invite students to tell what their movements mean. Encourage students to teach their movements to other classmates.

Shadow Plays

- cardboard box
- construction paper
- popsicle sticks
- crayons or markers
- glue
- scissors
- tracing paper
- flashlight or table lamp

Another form of drama performed to the accompaniment of the gamelan are shadow plays known as "wayang." Puppets are used to cast shadows on a large screen made of white cloth. The performances often portray the battle of good and evil in the lives of gods and heroes. Invite students to create stick puppets using popsicle sticks and construction paper and then put on an original shadow play. The puppets in a Balinese shadow play are elaborately decorated (even though the audience only sees their shadows) so that the performer can easily distinguish them.

To make a shadow box theatre, cut the flaps off the top of a cardboard box and cut out the bottom to look like a TV. Tape tracing paper across the inside of the opening to make a screen. Shine the light from behind the box so the puppets' shadows are visible from the front. Invite a group of students to play their gamelan instruments to accompany the puppet performance.

My Grandpa and the Sea

Written and illustrated by Katherine Orr
Minneapolis: Carolrhoda, 1990

Synopsis

Lila's grandpa was a fisherman on the island of St. Lucia (LU▪sha). As times changed, Grandpa's canoe, made from the trunk of a giant tree, was no match for the fishing boats with powerful engines. The new technology began to deplete the supply of fish in the sea and forced Grandpa to find another way to make a living. In his search to remain true to his beliefs, Grandpa teaches Lila many lessons about the ways of the sea and the heart.

Background

St. Lucia is an almond-shaped island at the southern end of the Caribbean. As depicted by the author's beautiful illustrations, this island has a reputation for being one of the last unspoiled islands in the area. Katherine Orr and her husband have conducted much research on fisheries and have lived for many years on Caribbean islands.

Deepen Your Understanding

1. Times were changing in St. Lucia. Franklin's boat had a powerful engine, long lines, giant nets, and could hold many fish. Grandpa's boat was much smaller and less efficient. With this new technology came Grandpa's concern that the fish were

becoming scarce. Discuss the word "scarce" with your students and relate the environmental concern to one that might hit closer to home, such as water conservation, recycling programs, and so on. Help children see the wisdom in Grandpa's philosophy of taking only a plateful of something rather than coming "to God's table each with a wheelbarrow. . . ."

- Why was Grandpa worried about the new boats?
- Do you think the new boats were a good idea? Why or why not?
- Do you think the sea in St. Lucia could run out of fish?
- What do you think could be done so that wouldn't happen?
- What did Grandpa mean when he said the fishermen came "to God's table with a wheelbarrow instead of a plate?"
- Do you know of anything that is "scarce"?
- How can we help so that other things, like trees, animals, and so on, don't become scarce?

2. Grandpa "lost his heart" when he was unable to do what he loved. Point out how each person is unique and has talents that are best put to use doing certain tasks. In the Caribbean, common occupations include fishing and growing and harvesting sugarcane, coffee, tropical fruits, and spices.

- What do you think Grammy meant when she said that Grandpa "lost his heart"?
- Why do you think Grandpa was unhappy driving a taxi and working in a store?
- Where do you feel most comfortable or "at home"?
- What do you like to do the most?
- What are some things you have tried, but were not happy doing?

3. Lila learned many things from her Grandpa, including lessons about the heart. In many cultures, elders are respected for their wisdom and knowledge.

- What do you think the word "wise" means?
- Who do you think is wise?
- What have you learned from someone who is older than you?
- Have you learned any lessons about the heart? What?

4. Fishing is common in St Lucia because the people are so near the sea. Fish is commonly prepared by marinating it in lime juice and then grilling or frying it. Sometimes fish is covered with a creamy sauce made from coconut milk. Point out the relationship between geography and the occupations people have and the foods people eat.

- What would you like to be when you grow up?
- Have you ever been fishing?

- Would it be possible for you to fish where you live? Why or why not?
- What do you think Lila might be when she grows up? Why?
- What foods do you enjoy eating?
- Where do these foods come from?

Extend Your Experience

Making Seamoss Pudding

Seamoss Pudding	
• ³/₄ cup (200 ml) dried Irish moss	Soak Irish moss for 30 minutes in enough cold water to cover. Wash well, drain, and remove
• 1 quart (.95 l) whole milk	any foreign matter. Pour milk into the top of a double boiler. Then place the Irish moss in a
• 2 cups (500 ml) fresh strawberries (pureed)	square of cheesecloth (8" or 20.4 cm square). Tie up the ends of the cheesecloth and suspend the bag in the milk. Simmer for 30
• ½ cup (125 ml) honey	minutes. Press the bag against the side of the
• water	pan occasionally to release the gel. Stir
• cheesecloth	continually. Remove from heat and discard the
• pinch of sea salt	bag. Pour the milk mixture into a blender. Add
	the pureed strawberries, honey, and salt. Blend
	at high speed. Pour into dessert dishes. Cover
	tightly and refrigerate for several hours before
	serving.

Tropical Environment

- brightly colored construction paper
- fluorescent paint or crayons
- string
- scissors
- aquarium supplies (optional)

With its azure-green waters and palm-lined shores, St. Lucia's beauty is often described as breathtaking. St. Lucia's coasts are lined with coral reefs that provide homes for many brightly colored tropical fish. The entire island rarely cools below 70° F (21° C) and almost never reaches above 85° F (29° C).

Invite children to make their own tropical environment. Encourage students to draw pictures of brightly colored tropical fish on construction paper. Help children cut out the fish and suspend the fish from the classroom ceiling to create a tropical effect. If possible, invite students to take on the responsibility of maintaining a classroom aquarium or fish bowl.

Fancy Lady

- 8 ¹/₂" x 11" (21.7 cm x 28 cm) white drawing paper
- scissors
- crayons or markers
- glue
- stapler
- brightly colored toothpicks

Grandpa's "pride and joy" was his beautifully painted canoe, which he named "Fancy Lady." It was carved from the trunk of a tree that grew high in the mountains. Grandpa carefully caulked the canoe's planks and painted her annually so that her bright colors would gleam in the sun.

Invite students to make a paper canoe, decorate it with bright colors, and give it a special name. Have each student fold a sheet of white drawing paper in half widthwise and then unfold. Have students fold each end up to the center fold line and then refold the original crease. (The paper will be folded in fourths.) The folded edge will be the bottom of the canoe. Using scissors, help children round the ends of the canoe by trimming off the lower corners. Staple the round edges together on each end of the canoe. Using crayons or markers, invite students to decorate and name their canoes. Insert two toothpicks through the canoe to hold its mid-section open. Put a dot of glue where each toothpick inserts through the walls of the canoe to hold the toothpicks in place.

Ways to Save

Grandpa was worried that Franklin was taking more from the sea than God could provide. He worried that if fishermen were not careful, there would come a day when there would be no fish left to catch. Point out to children that paper is something we use very regularly in many ways. Invite children to think of the many types of paper they use (drawing paper, paper towels, tissues, and so on.) Ask students where they think paper comes from and if they think we will ever run out of paper. Grandpa knew that "if we give back something for everything we take, we will always meet with abundance." Encourage students to brainstorm a list of ways they can conserve paper so there will always be an abundant supply. Ask children in what ways they can "give back" when they use paper (recycle, plant more trees, and so on). To discover the importance of paper, try going without it for a day! Then begin a paper-recycling program in your classroom.

My Little Island

Written and illustrated by Frané Lessac
New York: Harper & Row, 1984

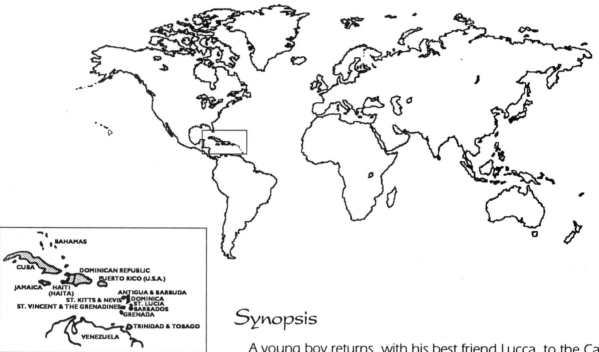

Synopsis

A young boy returns, with his best friend Lucca, to the Caribbean island where he was born. Together the boys experience tropical fruits, huge iguanas, barking frogs, and the calypso and reggae music of island life.

Background

The Caribbean islands stretch for about 2,000 miles from Florida to Venezuela. There are about thirty large islands and many smaller ones. The name "Caribbean" comes from the first people who lived on the islands. They were known as the "Caribs." There is incredible diversity in geography, race, and language among the islands.

Deepen Your Understanding

1. Houses in the Caribbean are often brightly painted, wooden structures. As described in the story, they "look like little rainbows sitting on the hills." The windows often have shutters, as depicted in the story illustrations, so rooms can be darkened during the heat of the day. The tin roof is peaked to shed heavy rains. Invite children to compare the houses in the story with their own homes.

- How would you describe the houses you see in the story?
- How are they different from your home? How are they the same?
- Why do you think houses in the Caribbean are brightly colored? What color would you paint your home? Why?
- Why do you think the doors and windows in the story are all open?

2. Review some of the names of the colorful and vibrant Caribbean flowers and trees (frangipani, red flamboyant trees, pink coral) as well as the more unusual animals (iguanas, barking frogs).

   - After seeing some Caribbean animals, why do you think Lucca and his friend said "Who will believe us back home?"
   - Would you believe someone who told you they saw a giant barking frog or a three-foot iguana? Why or why not?
   - The boys knew the names of only some of the trees and plants they saw. If you were showing a friend some trees and flowers where you live, which ones could you name?

3. Carnival is a celebration enjoyed throughout the Caribbean, but Trinidad's carnival has been acclaimed as one of the world's greatest spectacles. The celebration combines music and creative costumes as people parade through the streets for two days. Invite students to compare this festival with celebrations with which they are familiar.

   - What festivals do you celebrate in which costumes are worn? What do the costumes look like?
   - Have you ever seen a parade? How was it like the carnival in the story?
   - The two boys got to stay up late one night to enjoy the festivities. Have you ever gotten to stay up late for a special occasion?

4. The Caribbean markets, alive with colors, sights, smells, and noises, are very exciting. The Caribbean has fruit in abundance. Fine weather all year round guarantees a constant supply of a variety of fruits. Some fruits, such as mangoes, bananas, and citrus fruits, are exported and can be found in our markets. More fragile fruits, such as pawpaws and soursops, do not travel as easily. Show a sample of some tropical fruits that are available in your area.

   - The boys bought guavas, mangoes, and coconuts. What are your favorite fruits to eat?
   - Have you ever eaten any of the fruits the boys bought? Did you like the fruit?
   - Which tropical fruits would you like to try?

Extend Your Experience

Making Pumpkin Soup

When Lucca sampled some of the new Caribbean foods, he made funny faces. Ask children what new foods they have tried recently and if they made a funny face. Remind children that although Lucca was unsure how the new foods would taste, he did try them all. Make pumpkin soup with your class and enjoy a new taste.

Pumpkin Soup	
• 2 egg yolks (beaten)	Blend the cream and egg yolks and set
• 2 cups (500 ml) pumpkin filling	aside. Mix the pumpkin filling and consommé in a saucepan over medium
• 1 10-oz (300 ml) can beef consommé soup	heat. Stir constantly until mixture boils. Add cream and egg mixture to
• ½ cup (125 ml) heavy cream	saucepan and stir briskly until soup thickens. (Do not boil.) Season with
• salt	spices and remove from heat. Serve
• pepper	immediately.
• 1 tsp (5 ml) onion powder	
• dash of nutmeg	

Island Life

- construction paper
- crayons or markers
- empty paper-towel rolls
- tape

This book shows illustrations of the daily life in the Caribbean islands. Review the illustrations in the book, pointing out to the children the details in each picture. Take particular note that there is no glass in the windows, there is an abundance of vegetation, and that clothing is light. Invite children to work in pairs or individually to make pictures of island life using crayons and markers. Fasten the pictures together to form one long strip. Tape the ends of the strip to a paper-towel roll. Roll the pictures around another paper-towel roll so only the first picture shows. Two children can roll the paper-towel rolls together (one rolling, one unrolling) so one picture of island life is viewed at a time.

A Visit Home

- 12" x 18" (30.6 cm x 45.9 cm) construction paper
- pencils
- crayons or markers

The young boy in the story enjoyed showing his best friend, Lucca, where he used to live. Lucca learned a lot about Caribbean life and experienced new sights, sounds, and tastes. Encourage children to think about what they would want to show Lucca if he visited their home. Invite children to make comparisons between Caribbean life and life in their city or town. For example, "When Lucca visited the Caribbean, he tasted pumpkin soup. If Lucca visited me he could taste . . . " or "In the Caribbean, Lucca heard calypso music. If Lucca visited me, he could hear . . ." Encourage each child to create a comparison between the two cultures by writing a similar sentence on a 12" x 18" (30.6 cm x 45.9 cm) sheet of construction paper and then illustrating it. Children can compare tastes, sights, sounds, and so on. Younger children can dictate their sentences as you record them on their illustrations.

Jumby

- chalk
- stones or beanbags
- *Hopscotch Around the World* by Mary D. Lankford (optional)

The two boys visited St. Christopher's school and stayed to listen to folktales and play games. They also had time to make more new friends. Jumby is a version of the familiar game of hopscotch played in Trinidad. Sylvester, Desmond, Simon, Sylvia, Glendina, and Althea might have enjoyed playing this game with their visiting friends.

Using chalk, draw a hopscotch pattern on a flat surface. The first player begins by throwing his or her marker (stone or beanbag) into box 1. The player then jumps over box 1 and into all the other boxes as he or she progresses to the end of the pattern and turns around. The player hops back and picks up the marker. The player then throws the marker into box 2 and repeats the jumping sequence being careful never to jump in a box that has a marker in it. The first player to get through the entire pattern without a mistake wins. For more information about Jumby and other international versions of hopscotch, see Mary Lankford's *Hopscotch Around the World* (see the bibliography on page 207).

How the Ox Star Fell from Heaven

Retold and illustrated by Lily Toy Hong
Morton Grove, Illinois: Albert Whitman & Company, 1991

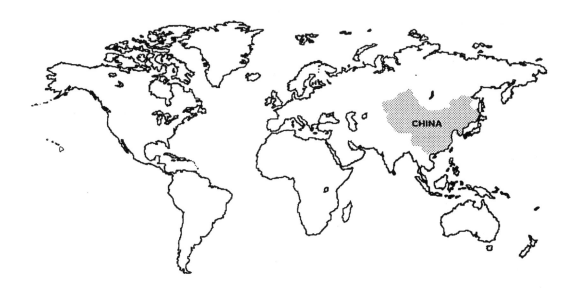

Synopsis

According to this Chinese tale, oxen once lived lives of luxury in the heavens. But after the Ox Star incorrectly delivered an important message, he was banished. The ox's blunder became the farmer's blessing. That is why today, oxen are a beast of burden.

Background

China is an agricultural country. Eighty percent of the population are engaged in agricultural work. Naturally, there are many folktales about farming and farm animals. For many years, oxen have been the main beast of burden on farmland in China. The author, Lily Toy Hong, grew up in a large Chinese-American family. She expanded the folktale on which this story is based.

Deepen Your Understanding

1. Folktales can add insight into the beliefs of a culture. The tales are often viewed as the mirror of a people. They are imaginative tales that often attempt to explain life's circumstances. Help children distinguish reality from make-believe in the story.

   - What parts of this story do you think are make-believe? Why?
   - What parts of the story do you think are real?

■ It is true that oxen are work animals. Do you think it is because of the Ox Star's mistake?

2. China was ruled by emperors for more than 2,000 years. In 1911,
   the last emperor was overthrown. The Forbidden City was once
   the home of China's emperors and ordinary people were not
   allowed inside. The buildings within this special "city" have yellow
   roofs because they once belonged to the emperor. In the past, no
   one but the emperor was allowed to use the color yellow. Point
   out the golden roof of the Imperial Palace in the story.

   ■ How does the emperor's palace look different from the
     houses the people lived in?
   ■ Why do you think the emperor was so important?
   ■ Do you know anyone who lives in a special house because
     he or she is very important? Who?

3. There was a time in China when the government wanted the
   people to wear neutral-colored clothing that looked almost like a
   uniform. Now, the Chinese wear whatever they want, but the
   traditional dark-colored "uniform" is still common among some
   adults. Invite children to compare the emperor's clothing with the
   people's clothing.

   ■ Why do you think the people in the story are all dressed
     alike?
   ■ Do you like to dress like your friends or do you like to look
     different?
   ■ How is the emperor's clothing different from the other
     people's clothing?
   ■ How is the clothing you see in the story different from your
     clothing? How is it the same?

4. There are many grain crops grown in China. The main crop in the
   north is wheat. The main crop in the south is rice. So the people
   who live in southern China are the "rice-eating" people. They eat
   steamed rice, rice-flour noodles, and rice gruel.

   ■ Have you ever been to a Chinese restaurant? Were you
     served rice?
   ■ What is your favorite Chinese food?
   ■ What is your favorite way to eat rice?
   ■ Do you think you would ever get tired of eating rice?
   ■ How many different types of rice dishes have you eaten
     (steamed rice, rice cakes, Rice Krispies, and so on)?

Extend Your Experience

Rice with Chopsticks

■ cooked rice
■ chopsticks

China has more people to feed than any other country in the world. Many of the people in China earn their living by farming. Chinese farmers plant rice seeds in small plots of ground called "seedbeds." These seedbeds are flooded with water and the plants are allowed to grow for about one month. Then the baby plants are moved to a larger field which is also then flooded. When the plants are fully grown, the water is drained off and the crop is harvested. Make some warm rice for your students to enjoy as you describe the growing process. Invite students to try eating with chopsticks. Students may find it a bit difficult at first, so encourage them to keep trying.

Smooth as Silk

- silk fabric swatches
- assorted fabric swatches
- paper bag

The oxen who lived in the Imperial Palace were clothed in the robes of the finest silk. The Chinese are famous for the quality and beauty of their silk fabrics. In fact, for many years, the Chinese alone knew that silk was made from the cocoons of tiny silkworms. About 8 to 9 days after a silkworm has spun a cocoon, the cocoons are unwound by hand. Each cocoon is made of a thread that is over 200 feet long. About 5 to 8 of these fine threads are twisted together to make one thread. The silk threads are then woven into cloth.

Bring in several swatches of fabric, including silk. Invite students to compare the textures. Put several swatches of fabric in a paper bag. Invite students to identify the silk swatch by using only their sense of touch.

Making Chinese Sweet Cakes

Because of Ox's mistake, the peasants enjoyed warm rice, tender vegetables, and Chinese sweet cakes three times a day. These sweet cakes are baked in molds and coated with an egg-yolk glaze to give them a shiny look. The traditional sweet cakes, also called "moon cakes," are quite difficult to make. But your students might enjoy this cookie version of a Chinese sweet cake. Make these cakes with your class and enjoy.

Chinese Sweet Cakes

• 1 cup (250 ml) softened butter	Cream butter and gradually add sugar. Blend in the vanilla and almonds. Slowly
• ½ cup (125 ml) powdered sugar	knead in the flour. Refrigerate the dough until chilled. Then roll the dough out on a
• 2 tsp (10 ml) vanilla	floured surface and cut into cookie
• 1 cup (250 ml) ground blanched almonds	shapes. Bake on a greased cookie sheet at 350°F (180°C) for 15 minutes.
• 1 ½ cups (375 ml) flour	

Chinese Farmer's Hat

- bamboo or pictures of bamboo
- construction paper or tagboard
- stapler
- yarn
- hole punch
- crayons or paint

The farmers in the story are wearing traditional Chinese hats to protect them from the sun while working in the fields. These hats are made from woven bamboo and are called "nung fu mao." If possible, display pictures of bamboo or have bamboo and authentic hats available. Children can make similar hats by making a cut from the edge to the center of an 18" (45.9 cm) circle of construction paper or tagboard. Overlap the edges about four inches (10.2 cm) and staple the rim edges together. Punch a hole on each side of the hat and tie a piece of yarn through each hole. Children can use crayons or paint to color their hats to resemble the shade of bamboo.

Our Home Is the Sea

Written by Riki Levinson and illustrated by Dennis Luzak
New York: E.P. Dutton, 1988

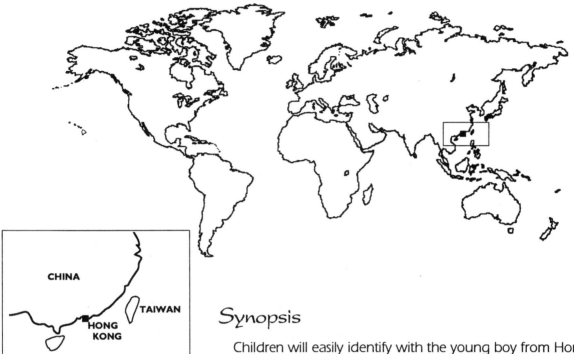

Synopsis

Children will easily identify with the young boy from Hong Kong who longs to leave school behind and spend time fishing with his grandfather. This modern-day child desires to follow the traditions of his father and grandfather.

Background

Before writing and illustrating this book, both the author and the artist traveled to Hong Kong to fully understand the city's colors, noises, and crowds. The author, Riki Levinson, found that the Chinese living in Hong Kong were very similar to her own family. Hong Kong is a British colony, although almost all of the people who live there are Chinese.

Deepen Your Understanding

1. Hong Kong is one of the world's most crowded places. There are many high-rise buildings because much of the land is too wet or hilly to build on. Some families wait many years to get such an apartment as pictured in the story. Washed clothes are often hung out the apartment windows to save space indoors.

   ▪ Have you ever been in a very crowded place? How could you tell it was crowded?

- How is the apartment in the picture the same or different from places you have seen or lived in?
- The little boy in the story said he would not like to live in a "tall house." Would you? Why or why not?

2. There are many parks throughout Hong Kong and the people there enjoy them in many ways. It is not unusual to see caged birds in the park. Each morning, bird owners take the birds to the park and enjoy their singing while they talk to their friends. Others practice T'ai Chi. T'ai Chi is a form of exercise that includes circular hand movements and intricate foot patterns. It emphasizes gentle force and inner harmony.

- What are some things the little boy saw in the park as he walked through it?
- Have you ever seen these things in a park where you live? What have you seen at a park?
- How did the boy respond to the things the people were doing? What would you do if you saw people doing similar things in your park?

3. Hong Kong has many rivers which serve as home to millions who live on boats. The hundreds of boats cluster together to form floating cities. "Sampans" are moved up and down the river by poling. A stick or pole is stuck into the ground and pushed while walking along the side or catwalk of the boat.

- The little boy was anxious to get on the houseboat with his family. Have you ever been on a boat? Did it look like the boats in the story? How was it the same or different?
- How would living on a boat be different from living in a house or apartment?
- Which would you like better? Why?

4. The author gives insight into how the little boy really feels by describing his emotions. The little boy "couldn't wait" for school to be out. He also wished for peacock feathers and that he could be a fisherman one day. Help children understand that although this little boy lives many miles away, he is very much like them in many ways.

- Why was the boy in such a hurry?
- Have you ever been so anxious for something to happen that you just "couldn't wait"? When?
- The little boy wished he didn't have to go to school. He also wished that he had peacock feathers and that he could be a fisherman one day. What do you wish for?

Extend Your Experience

Tea Tasting

- loose tea or teabags
- teapot
- cups

Tea is an important part of the Chinese way of life. In the story, the young boy's mother served tea and congee (thin rice soup). There are many kinds of Chinese tea, but they can be grouped into three major types—green, black, and oolong. Jasmine is a mild green tea and one of the most common. The Chinese usually drink their tea plain without sugar, lemon, or cream.

Prepare several pots of tea for your students to sample. Measure loose tea into a teapot. Use one teaspoon of tea for each cup of water or suit to taste. Or, you many want to use teabags. Pour boiling water into the teapot. Cover the teapot and teabags and let stand for a few minutes. Pour tea directly into cups. Serving tea to guests while visiting is an important social event in Chinese life.

Patient Proverbs

- drawing paper
- crayons or markers

Ask children to identify actions or words from the story that indicate the little boy's impatience. For example, he ran to the tram, hurried down the stairs, and could not wait for the light to turn green. Chinese proverbs are learned as a way of expressing a truth or to explain an important lesson. There are many Chinese proverbs about the virtue of patience. Children may be familiar with some proverbs about patience, such as "A watched pot never boils" or "Haste makes waste." Share the following Chinese proverbs about patience with your students.

"A person in haste cannot eat warm bean curd."
(Since bean curd making takes some time, one cannot have it if he or she is impatient.)
"A person cannot become fat with just one mouthful of food."
(This proverbs means that one cannot become successful with just one try. A person must be patient and continue to try and try again until he or she succeeds.)
Invite students to draw a picture illustrating a time when they were not patient. Encourage students to write or dictate one of the Chinese proverbs about patience beneath the picture as a reminder.

Fish Catch

- construction paper
- paper clips
- scissors
- string
- magnets
- tuna
- crackers

Fish is an important food for the Chinese living in Hong Kong. Give students an opportunity to imagine they are fishermen just as the little boy in the story so much wanted to be. Invite children to draw many different sizes of fish on paper. Help children cut out the fish and attach a paper clip to each fish's mouth. Tie a magnet (hook) to the end of a length of string (fishing line). Children can "catch" the fish by dropping the magnet near a fish's mouth. After all the fish are caught, spread some tuna on crackers and enjoy your catch! If possible, visit a nearby fish market.

T'ai Chi

- music (optional)

Physical fitness is important in everyday life in China and Hong Kong. As illustrated in the story, people often practice T'ai Chi in the park. The movements are very slow and involve all parts of the body, incorporating both balance and muscle control. It is a very popular exercise which can relax the mind as well as the body. Invite your students to try these simple T'ai Chi movements.

Stand erect, hands easily at sides, palms back. Heels are together, toes slightly apart. Sinking slightly with soft knees, shift weight onto right foot and step with left foot (toes straight forward) to the left side so that feet are shoulder-width apart. Distribute weight evenly on both feet. Let arms rise upward to shoulder height in front. Draw wrists toward shoulders, fingers slightly straightening. Continue circular movement, gently pressing hands down to sides again. The body rises slightly with arms and sinks again as arms return to sides. To encourage slow steady movement, play appropriate music.

The River Dragon

Written by Darcy Pattison and illustrated by Jean and Mou-Sien Tseng
New York: Lothrop, Lee & Shepard, 1991

Synopsis

Ying Shao must cross the River Dragon's bridge to attend a customary banquet held by his Bride-to-Be's family. Swallows are served as the main course and it is common knowledge that dragons love swallows. How will Ying Shao get back across the bridge and safely past the River Dragon with swallows on his breath?

Background

The dragon is a symbol of China, but it also has many other symbolic meanings. According to ancient legend, the dragon is the god of rain. It is believed that dragons live in seas, rivers, and lakes and are responsible for rainfall. Darcy Pattison drew on authentic details of Chinese dragon lore when she created this original folktale.

Deepen Your Understanding

1. Ying Shao feared the River Dragon and offered a gift each time he crossed the bridge in an attempt to assure his safety. Even the River Dragon, though dragons are "very brave folk," had some fears. The dragon was afraid of centipedes and five-colored scarves. Invite children to share their own fears as they relate to the characters in the story.

- Would you have been afraid if you had to cross the River Dragon's bridge? Why or why not?
- What are you afraid of?
- Do you think Ying Shao was brave? Why or why not?
- Do you consider yourself to be brave?

2. The River Dragon's demise came as a result of his greed. Though he had a beautiful pearl, he risked losing it to gain what he thought was a pearl even larger and more beautiful.

- If you had been the River Dragon, would you have tried to get the Night-Shining Pearl or would you have kept the pearl you had in your claw? Why?
- Have you ever wanted something that seemed to be better than what you had? Did you get it? How did you feel?
- What do you think Ying Shao will do with Ti-Lung's pearl?
- What does it mean to be greedy?

3. Invite children to take a closer look at the picture in the story that illustrates all the guests seated around a table full of delicious food. Point out that the classic Chinese table is round to allow guests to be at equal distances from the food. The respected person (usually the eldest) is seated at the place of honor, which is usually at the north end of the table. Each place setting has a plate, a bowl, chopsticks, and sauces. Invite children to notice

some of the other delicious dishes set before the guests at the banquet. Besides the swallow dish, the guests might be eating hot and sour soup, bao zi (steamed stuffed bun), and shrimp with vegetables.

- What is your favorite dinner dish?
- How does this scene look different from what your home might look like at dinnertime? How is it the same?
- Which of these Chinese dishes would you like to try?
- Do you have a special place you always sit at your dinner table?

4. The clothing in the story is traditional Chinese. Clothes are made of silk or cotton. The men usually wear plain costumes with fewer patterns, while women wear colorful costumes with more intricate designs. If you visited China today, you would not see people dressed like this except for special occasions.

- How would you describe the clothing you see in the story?
- How is it different from your own clothing?
- Which would you like to wear? Why?
- Do you wear special clothing for special occasions? What?

Extend Your Experience

Dragon Hunt

- animal pictures
- glue
- construction paper
- *Emma's Dragon Hunt* by Catherine Stock
- lined paper
- pencil

Ask students to describe what the dragon in the story looked like. Point out that Chinese mythical dragons were often depicted as being parts of many different animals put together. The River Dragon had the head of a camel, horns of a deer, eyes of a demon, ears of an ox, neck of a snake, scales of a carp, palms of a tiger, and claws of a hawk. Provide children will pictures of animals cut from magazines. Invite children to use an assortment of animal parts to create their own mythical dragon creatures. Display the pictures around the room.

Then read *Emma's Dragon Hunt* by Catherine Stock (see the bibliography on page 208). Invite students to imagine that their dragon has gotten lost and they are going on a hunt to find it. Invite students to write or dictate a description of their dragons. For example, a child might describe his or her dragons as having the head of an elephant, the neck of a giraffe, and the eyes of an eagle. Invite each child to read or tell about his or her dragon. Challenge other students to "hunt" for the picture that matches the description.

Making Bao Zi

The goldsmith boasted that his wife was an excellent cook. Kal-Li's mother had many special recipes for swallow dishes. Invite students to notice the round, white bread on the table in the banquet illustration. This Chinese steamed, stuffed dumpling is called "bao zi." It is a popular Chinese favorite. Make bao zi with your students.

Bao Zi	
• bread dough	Chop the cabbage into pieces and squeeze
• 1 lb (450 g) Chinese cabbage	out the juice. Chop a few green onions and a small amount of gingerroot. Combine the
• 1 lb (450 g) ground pork or beef	ground pork or beef, chopped cabbage, green onions, gingerroot, sesame oil, soy sauce,
• green onions	and salt in a bowl. Then cut the bread dough
• gingerroot	into small pieces. Roll each piece into a flat
• 2 Tbsp (30 ml) sesame oil	circle. Place a spoonful of the mixture in the center of each dough circle. Bring the edges
• 2 Tbsp (30 ml) soy sauce	to the center and pinch tightly to seal. Steam the dumplings for 10 to 15 minutes in
• ½ tsp (2.5 ml) salt	a steamer. (Or, they can be fried for 7 to 10 minutes.) Enjoy! Invite students to share
	some of their family's special recipes with
	the class.

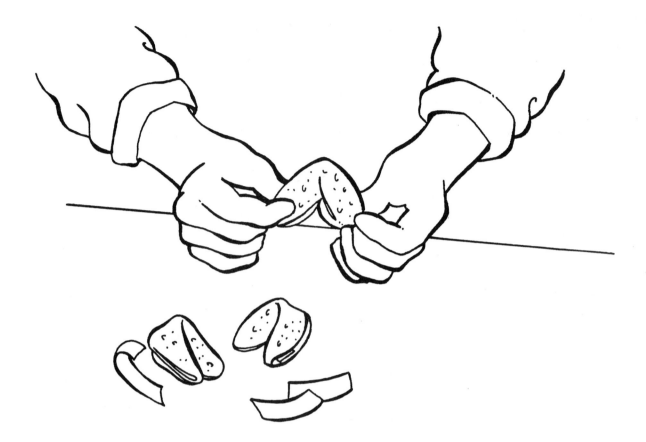

Making Fortune Cookies

Fortune cookies are often the last course of a Chinese-American meal. They are served as a dessert. Make personalized fortune cookies with your students.

Fortune Cookies	
• 1 lb (450 g) wheat flour	Combine the flour, sugar, and sesame oil.
• 3 tsp (15 ml) sesame oil	Gradually add water until the flour mixture is a doughy consistency and easy
• 3 tsp (15 ml) sugar	to handle. Separate the dough into small
• water	pieces. Roll the pieces into flat circles
• small slips of paper	about 3 inches (7.6 cm) in diameter. Bring
	both sides of the circles together and
	pinch the edges closed. Leave small
	openings to insert the fortunes after
	baking. Fold the center of the half-circle
	shapes in half slightly to make a tradi-
	tional fortune cookie shape. Bake the
	cookies at 350°F (180°C) for 5 to 10
	minutes.

Looking for a Friend

Ying Shao would probably have liked to have had a friend go with him as he crossed the River Dragon's bridge. Perhaps if Ying Shao had played this popular Chinese singing game, the dragon might have had a different attitude towards him.

Invite students to stand in a circle with one child in the center. Encourage everyone to join in singing the song and clapping their hands while the child in the center walks around looking for a "new friend." When the children sing the words, "Give a salute and let's shake hands," the child in the center stops in front of a new friend. The two children bow their heads and shake hands with one another. The new friend then becomes the child in the center. Give each student an opportunity to find a new friend.

The Bird Who Was an Elephant

Written by Aleph Kamal and illustrated by Frané Lessac
New York: Lippincott, 1989

Synopsis

A little bird flies in from the desert to take in all the sights and sounds of a busy village in India. He admires the beautifully colored saris worn by the women at the river, he breathes in the wonderful smells of the spice shop, and he seeks the wisdom of a Palmist, who tells him what he once was and will be in the future. On his way home, he experiences even more aspects of village life. After a full and adventurous day, the tired bird is glad to return to his home in the desert.

Background

India is a large country in southern Asia. It has the second largest population of any country in the world, yet is only about one-third the size of the United States. Only China has more people. Aleph Kamal grew up in North Africa and India. This book is a result of his desire to write a story about India so children in the West would have a better understanding of the Eastern world.

Deepen Your Understanding

1. As Bird flew over the city, he saw many sights and heard many sounds. He saw women in their beautifully colored saris and smelled the aroma coming from the spice shop. He saw a Sacred

Cow with a garland of orange marigolds around its neck and a Snake Charmer. Invite children to recall other sights and sounds described in the story and then compare them to the city or town in which they live.

- What do you think was the most interesting sight Bird saw as he flew over the city in India?
- What three things would Bird have seen if he flew over your city or town?
- What do you think people who live in India would think is the most interesting sight in your city?
- If you could show Bird a wonderful thing about your city or town, what would it be?

2. "Tiffin" is the word used in India to mean a light lunch or snack. The workers from the rice fields were having a quick tiffin of samosas and bhajis in the afternoon. A "tiffin carrier" is made up of three or four round metal boxes all clipped together with a handle on the top. (There is a picture of a tiffin carrier in the book *Everybody Cooks Rice* by Norah Dooley, also listed in this resource.) Many office workers in Bombay have their lunch sent to them from their homes by tiffin carriers. Many people earn their living by providing this "meals-on-wheels" service.

- Samosas and bhajis are both snacks made with vegetables. Do you ever eat vegetables for a snack?
- If you were going to have a snack, what would you eat? Do you think the people living in India might have the same snack? Why or why not?
- What do you use to carry food in?
- Would you like the job of delivering lunches? Why or why not?

3. The number of cattle in India is enormous. As depicted in the story, the cow is considered sacred. Cows are allowed to roam the streets freely and are a symbol of the sacredness of all life. Explain to students the meaning of the word "sacred" (highly valued, important, worthy of respect). Encourage students to describe what is sacred to them.

- What does "sacred" mean?
- How do you think cows are treated in India?
- What is sacred to you?
- How do you treat what is really important to you?

4. Hinduism, India's oldest religion, is practiced by over eighty percent of the people living in India. Hindus believe that when a person's body dies, his or her soul is reborn into another body, either human or animal. This is why the palmist told Bird that he had been an Elephant many years ago and that he would soon become a Fish.

- If someone were able to tell you something about your future, what would you like to know?

- How do you think Bird's life will be different if he becomes a Fish?
- If you could come back in another life, what would you like to be? Why?

Extend Your Experience

Spice Sampler

- variety of spices (cloves, cinnamon, nutmeg, mace, mustard, cumin, turmeric, fennel, coriander, ginger)
- opaque film canisters
- paper
- pencils

Bird perched over the spice shop and enjoyed breathing in the many wonderful smells. Visiting a spice shop in an Indian town is a truly unique experience. Spices are sold as powder or as whole seeds. The spices give cooked food a unique taste and flavor.

Before beginning this activity, make some small holes in the top of several opaque film canister lids. (A heated nail slides through the plastic lid very easily.) The holes should be small enough so students cannot peek through them, but large enough to allow the aroma of what is inside to escape. Your nearest photo-developing store is an excellent source of film canisters. They are usually more than willing to allow you to "recycle" the unwanted canisters. Fill each canister with a different spice and number each canister. Invite students to smell each spice and record the numbers of the three spices they like best.

After each student has had a chance to smell all of the spices, make a bar graph on the chalkboard showing the results. List the number of each spice container along the bottom of the graph and the number of students who chose it as their favorite along the left side of the graph. After the favorites are recorded, reveal the name of each spice. Give students a chance to smell their favorites again and to mentally match the name with the smell. Try the smelling activity again on another day and challenge students to play "Name That Spice."

Making East Indian Tea

India is the leading producer and exporter of tea in the world. Tea earns the country a valuable income. Tea, with lots of milk and sugar, is a common drink enjoyed by East Indian people. Give your students an opportunity to enjoy some delicious tea.

East Indian Tea

• 1 pint (½ l) water • 4 tsp (20 ml) tea leaves • 8 tsp (40 ml) sugar • ½ cup (125 ml) milk • 1 tsp (5 ml) ginger • 8 to 10 cardamom seeds (crushed)	Heat the water, tea leaves, sugar, and milk in a saucepan. Add the crushed cardamom seeds and ginger. Remove the pan from the heat as soon as the tea comes to a boil. Strain the mixture into a teapot for serving. Serve the tea in small cups or saucers.

Making Samosas

In the story, the workers in the rice fields were enjoying a snack that included samosas. Samosas are small pastries filled with peas and potatoes. Invite the children to help you make this popular snack.

Samosas 1

- 2 cups (500 g) flour
- 4 Tbsp (60 ml) vegetable oil
- 6 Tbsp (90 ml) and ⅓ cup (90 ml) water, divided
- 1 ¾ lb (750 g) potatoes
- 1 ⅔ cups (430 ml) frozen peas
- 2 Tbsp (30 ml) vegetable oil
- 2 tsp (10 ml) cumin seeds
- 1 medium onion (finely chopped)
- 1 ½" (4 cm) fresh ginger root
- 4 fresh hot green chile peppers

- 1 tsp (5 ml) salt
- 1 tsp (5 ml) cayenne pepper
- ⅔ cup (180 ml) fresh coriander leaves (chopped)
- vegetable oil for deep-frying

Make a pastry by adding 4 Tbsp (60 ml) vegetable oil to the flour until it resembles fine bread crumbs. Slowly add the water to make a stiff dough. Place the dough in an oiled plastic bag and let it rest for 30 minutes. Meanwhile, make the filling. Heat 2 Tbsp (30 ml) oil and add the cumin seeds.

2

Add the chopped onion and ginger. Cook until the ingredients begin to soften. Cut the potatoes into small cubes and remove the seeds from the peppers. Then cut the chile peppers into thin rings and add the rings and the potatoes to the onion mixture. Stir in the salt and about ⅓ cup (90 ml) of water. Cover and let simmer until the potatoes are cooked. Add the frozen peas and let the mixture cook for 4 more minutes. Stir in the cayenne pepper and coriander. Allow to cool. Roll out the dough and cut into 18 large circles. Cut each circle in half and fold to form a cone. Seal the long edges with water. Use a fork to press down the seams. Fill the cones with the potato mixture. Seal the tops of the cones and deep-fry the samosas until they are golden brown. Enjoy!

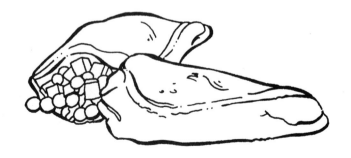

Chilly

- chalk
- markers, such as stones or beanbags
- *Hopscotch Around the World* by Mary D. Lankford (optional)

As Bird flew in from the desert in India, he looked down onto the city and saw many colorful sights. If Bird had flown over an area where children were playing, he might have seen a large square divided into four equal squares drawn in the soft red-clay earth. Children in India use this pattern to play a version of hopscotch they call "chilly."

Using chalk, draw the four-square pattern on a flat surface. The first player throws his or her marker into the first box (left-hand box closest to player). The player then hops into that box with one foot. Using the hopping foot, the player kicks the marker into the next box. The player then hops into that box and kicks the marker into the next box. The player continues until he or she completes all four boxes or the marker lands on or goes out of the boundary lines. The play continues with the player throwing the marker into the second box and hopping through the pattern (skipping the first box by jumping over it). The first player to successfully pass his or her marker through the pattern beginning with each of the four boxes as a starting point is the winner.

Potato Pancakes All Around: A Hanukkah Tale

Written and illustrated by Marilyn Hirsh
New York: Bonim Books, 1978

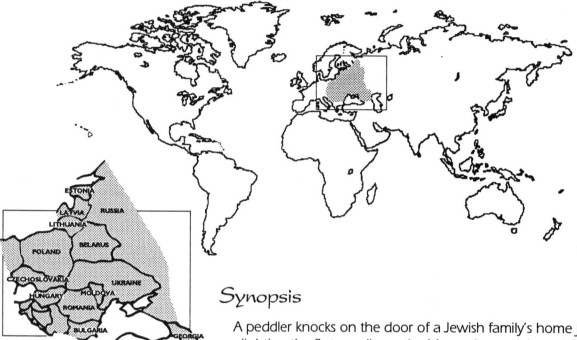

Synopsis

A peddler knocks on the door of a Jewish family's home just as they are lighting the first candle on the Menorah to celebrate Hanukkah. Welcomed with open arms, the peddler accepts the family's invitation to join them. The fun begins when the peddler sets out to prove he can make delicious potato pancakes from a simple crust of bread.

Background

People of the Jewish faith live in over 120 countries around the world. Hanukkah, also called "the Festival of Lights," is an important winter holiday. It celebrates the miracle of the holy oil that unexpectedly burned in the Temple for eight days after the Maccabees defeated the Syrians. The Syrians tried to destroy the Jewish way of life. This eight-day celebration is a joyous holiday filled with games, special foods, gifts, singing, and dancing.

Deepen Your Understanding

1. Hanukkah is the Jewish holiday which provides the story line for *Potato Pancakes All Around*. Many other holidays, such as Sukkot (harvest festival), Rosh Hashanah (New Year), and Yom Kippur (Day of Atonement), are also celebrated. Invite children to compare the holiday festivities in the story with holidays they celebrate.

- What holiday do you most enjoy celebrating? Why?
- The family enjoyed eating potato pancakes to celebrate Hanukkah. What is your favorite holiday food?
- The children played with a dreidel. Do you have a special holiday game you enjoy playing? What?
- What special things do you do to prepare for a holiday?

2. Invite children to look closely at the illustration in the story of the family sitting around the dinner table. The father is serving drinks from a samovar. A samovar can heat liquid and keep it warm. The lamp on the table is fueled by kerosene. The small handle between the two glass bowls adjusts the height of the flame. Invite children to compare this dinner table scene with a dinner table scene at their home.

   - How does this dinner table look different from your dinner table at home? How is it the same?
   - Have you ever eaten potato pancakes? What have you eaten that is made from potatoes?
   - Would you like to try potato pancakes? Why or why not?
   - What else does it look like the family might be eating?

3. Male members of a Jewish family sometimes wear "yarmulkes" (YAH■muh■kuhz) or skull caps to show respect for God. Married women also cover their heads out of modesty and respect. As depicted in the story, women often wore dresses which covered them from neck to ankle and had long sleeves and aprons.

   - How are the clothes in the story different from your clothes? How are they the same?
   - Why do you think the Jews in the story covered their heads out of respect for God? What is respect?
   - What do the clothes in the pictures tell you about the people in the story? What do your clothes tell about you?

4. Jews all over the world celebrate Hanukkah by lighting the Menorah. On the first night, the shamash (helper candle) is used to light one candle. Each night one more candle is added and lit. It is customary to light the Menorah in the window so that all who pass by can see it and know which night of Hanukkah it is. Encourage children to think about winter holidays that include candles or lights.

   - What are some winter holidays you celebrate or know about?
   - Can you think of any other winter holidays that include candles or lights? Why might you see a lot of lights as decorations in the winter?
   - How does seeing candles and lights outside make you feel on a winter night?
   - How did people light and warm their houses before electricity?
   - When was the last time you saw a lit candle?

Extend Your Experience

Dreidel

- 3" (7.6 cm) squares of tagboard
- markers
- pencils
- beans, buttons, or other small items for tokens

After the family enjoyed the best potato pancakes ever, they danced, sang, and played games. As illustrated in the story, the children played with a dreidel (DRAY•dl). A dreidel is a spinning top that has four Hebrew letters on it. These letters are the initials for Nes Gadol Hayah Sham which means "a great miracle happened here." Invite each child to make a dreidel using a tagboard square and a pencil. Help children write one Hebrew letter on each edge of the square.

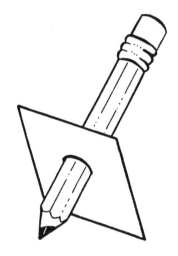

Nun   Gimel   Hay   Shin

Carefully push a short pencil through the center of each of the tagboard squares. Divide children into small groups to play the dreidel game. Each group needs only one dreidel, but each child needs an equal amount of tokens (beans, buttons, or other small items). Before the first child spins the dreidel, each child puts one token in the "pot." If the dreidel stops with Nun at the top, the player takes nothing from the pot. If Gimel lands at the top, the player takes all of the tokens. If Hay lands at the top, the player takes half of what is in the pot. If Shin lands on top, the player puts one token into the pot. Each player puts another token in the pot before the next player takes his or her spin. The game continues until one person has all of the tokens.

Making Potato Pancakes

Potato pancakes, or "latkes," are one of the most traditional of all Hanukkah foods. They are fried in oil to remind the Jewish people of the oil that burned in the Temple for eight days when it should have lasted only one day. Make potato pancakes with your class to enjoy using Grandma Yetta's and Grandma Sophie's recipe in the back of *Potato Pancakes All Around*. Latkes are often served with sour cream and applesauce.

Around We Go

- "Around We Go," *Learning by Doing, Dancing, and Discovering #76*, Educational Activities (or any music with a 2/4 tempo)

In this Hanukkah tale, the family enjoys eating, playing games, singing, and dancing together. Teach your students this simple Israeli circle dance called "Around We Go." Begin the dance with students joining hands in a single circle facing center.

Counts	Steps
8	Introduction (wait in place)
16	1. Circle L (CW) walking Moving CW, take 16 walking steps beginning on L. End facing center and drop hands. (Use other basic movements such as sliding, tiptoeing, or skipping each time the dance repeats.)
16	2. Squat and Up Squat (2 cts) and get up (2 cts). Repeat (4 cts). Squat and hold (4 cts) and get up and hold (4 cts).
4	3. Interlude Mark time in place RLRL before beginning dance again.

Menorah

- 9" x 12" (22.9 cm x 30.6 cm) construction paper
- 5" x 1/2" (12.7 cm x 1.2 cm) strips of construction paper for "candles"
- small yellow construction-paper triangles for "flames"
- glue

Lighting the Menorah is the central ritual in the Hanukkah celebration. The candles are traditionally placed in the Menorah from right to left and lit from left to right so the newest is always lit first. The shamash is usually higher than, or set apart from, the rest of the candles and is used to light them.

Invite the children to make their own Menorahs to celebrate Hanukkah in the classroom. Have students place a 9" x 12" (22.9 cm x 30.6 cm) piece of construction paper horizontally on their desks. Give each student nine candle strips. Invite students to glue the candle strips in a row across their papers, beginning on the right. Be sure students place one candle a bit higher than the rest to represent the shamash. Have students "light" the Menorah by gluing a small yellow triangle flame on top of each candle on each night of Hanukkah, beginning on the left.

The Day of Ahmed's Secret

Written by Florence Parry Heide and Judith Heide Gilliland and illustrated by Ted Lewin
New York: Lothrop, Lee & Shepard, 1990

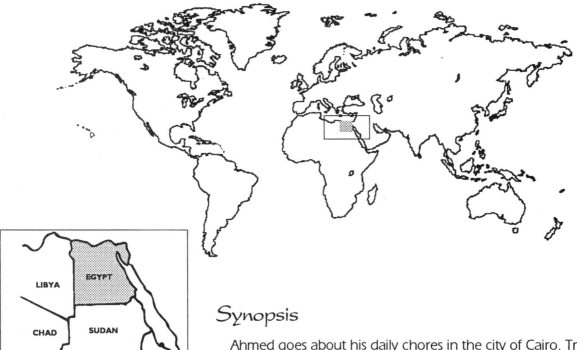

Synopsis

Ahmed goes about his daily chores in the city of Cairo. Traveling through the noisy, crowded city in his delivery cart, Ahmed is preoccupied with the intense loudness of his silent secret. At sundown when his work is finished, he stands before his family anxious to reveal his special secret—he has learned to write his name in Arabic.

Background

Though pyramids and mummies in museums may be the first thoughts children have of ancient Egypt, there is far more to know and understand about the Egyptian world today. Egypt, which is located in Africa, is a beautiful land of clear blue skies and bright sunshine. Judith Heide Gilliland lived in the Middle East for five years. Two of those years she spent in Cairo. Ted Lewin has traveled all over the world to gather material for his illustrations.

Deepen Your Understanding

1. Ahmed had a secret. Most children will identify with Ahmed's experience of keeping a secret or eagerly waiting to share a secret with someone. Take the opportunity to point out this similarity that the children and Ahmed share.

- Ahmed described his secret as being like a friend to him. What do you think he means?
- Ahmed also said that above all the noise in the city, the loudest sound of all was the silence of his secret. How can the silent sound of a secret be loud?
- With whom do you share secrets?
- What was Ahmed's secret? Why do you suppose Ahmed was so pleased with his secret?

2. Besides the many sounds Ahmed heard in the city, there were many interesting sights as well. Turn through the pages of the book once again and encourage children to notice unique features of Cairo and its people. Point out some of the architectural features of the crowded city. In many buildings of the old sections of Cairo, open-front shops occupy the ground floors and small apartments make up the upper floors. Cairo is well-known for its beautiful mosques, city walls, and gates.

- How are the buildings you see in the pictures different from buildings where you live? How are they the same?
- Would you like to visit Cairo? Why or why not?
- What do you think is the most beautiful building where you live?

3. In Arab capitals, such as Cairo, bazaars are permanent markets that are open every day. Stalls have been owned by the same family for generations. "Souq" (sook) is the Arabic word for "market," but it is said to have originally meant "street." Where there is a souq, there is always a street. An Arab souq consists of narrow alleys that weave among old houses and grand mosques. Both sides of the alley are crowded with stalls where goods overflow onto the pavement.

- How are the streets of Cairo different from the streets where you live?
- Have you ever been to an outdoor market? When? What did you see?
- What can you buy in Cairo that you could not buy where you live?

4. Ahmed closed his eyes to have a quiet time as his father had told him to do each day. Because the city is so noisy and crowded, finding a place to be alone and enjoy a quiet moment in Cairo is not easy to do.

- Ahmed's father told him that it was important to have "quiet spaces" in his head. What do you think Ahmed's father meant? Do you have quiet spaces in your head?
- Where is the noisiest place you have been?
- Where do you go when you want to be alone and quiet?
- What do you think Ahmed was thinking about when he was having his quiet time?
- What do you think about when you are alone?

Extend Your Experience

Sounds

The streets of Cairo were very crowded and noisy. Ask students to recall the sounds Ahmed heard as he went about his work. Ask students which sounds are ones they are not likely to hear as they walk down the street in their city or town. Encourage students to think of some sounds they hear that Ahmed would probably not hear in Cairo.

Ahmed created the sound "karink rink rink, karink rink rink" to describe his cart as it rolled down the bumpy street. Ask students to think of a chore they do each day. Encourage students to create a sound that best describes that action. Invite students to share their creative sounds with the class.

Hats-a-Plenty

- various types of hats
- *Hats Hats Hats* by Ann Morris

In very hot climates, such as Egypt, people have to protect themselves from the sun's powerful rays. Point out the types of head coverings illustrated in the story. The small hat Hassan is wearing is called a "talk•AY•uh." Women often drape scarves over their heads and around their necks, like the old woman leaning out of the window is wearing. Invite students to bring in a favorite or unusual hat from home to share with the class. Encourage children to explain why and when they wear their hats. Help children recognize that people all over the world wear head coverings. Share *Hats Hats Hats* by Ann Morris (see the bibliography on page 207) with your class.

Making Falafil

Hassan, the street vendor, gave Ahmed a dish of beans and noodles. Another popular dish sold by street vendors in Cairo is called "koh•share•EE." It is a tasty mixture of rice, lentils, macaroni, fried onions, and tomato sauce. Falafil is another popular favorite. Falafil is a mixture of beans, spices, and wheat germ. The mixture is combined with water and formed into small balls or patties and deep-fried. Make some falafil with your class using a prepared package mix. You can find the mix in a Middle Eastern market or at a health food store.

Falafil	
• falafil mix	Prepare the mix according to the directions
• pita pocket bread	on the package. Roll the falafil into small
• lettuce	balls and fry in oil. Place the falafil balls in
• tomatoes	pita pocket bread. Garnish with lettuce,
• sour cream or yogurt	tomatoes, and sour cream or yogurt. Enjoy!
• oil	

Arabic Lesson

- paper
- pencils

Arabic is the language of the Egyptians. Ahmed was very excited to show his family that he could write his name in Arabic. Point out to children that Arabic is not written with the same letters of the alphabet that we use. This language has its own sound symbols. And, Arabic is written and read from right to left rather than from left to right like English. Give children an opportunity to relate to Ahmed's feelings of pride and accomplishment by learning to write and say an Arabic word. "SHOH▪krun" means "thank you" in Arabic. It is written from right to left like this.

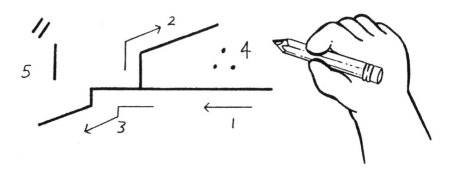

Encourage students to share the new word they have learned to write with their families, just as Ahmed did.

Floss

Written and illustrated by Kim Lewis
Cambridge, Massachusetts: Candlewick Press, 1992

Synopsis

Floss is a young Border collie who really knows how to play ball. But Floss must leave the town where she grew up to become a sheepdog on a distant farm in England. There is much work for her to do and her carefree days of playing with the children seem lost forever. That is, until the farmer realizes his children miss playing with Floss as much as she misses playing with them.

Background

England, Scotland, and Wales are the countries that make up Great Britain. Northern Ireland and Great Britain comprise the United Kingdom. The capital of the whole United Kingdom is London, England. Kim Lewis lives on a sheep farm in Northumberland, England, where this story is based.

Deepen Your Understanding

1. Great Britain is one of the world's most crowded countries and the largest percent of Great Britain's population lives in England. However, England also contains large areas of moorland and mountains, such as the heather-covered hills pictured in the story. Only ten percent of the people live in the countryside because there is little work to be found there.

- Floss, the old man, and the children lived in the valley where nothing much grew except sheep. How is this area different from where you live?
- Would you like to live in the country? Why or why not?
- Why do you think so few people live in the country in England?
- What kind of jobs can people do where Floss lived?

2. Like children all over the world, children in England are very fond of animals. About half of the families have a pet of some type, but dogs are a favorite. Dogs all over the world do some incredible jobs for people, just as Floss learned to do the important job of herding sheep. In some parts of the world, dogs pull sleds. Some dogs are hunting dogs and others do the important job of "seeing" for people who are blind.

- Do you think Floss' job of herding sheep was important? Why or why not?
- What other jobs can you think of that dogs do?
- Have you ever trained a dog to do something for you? What? Was it difficult?
- What do you think would be a good job to teach a dog? Why?

3. There are two kinds of sheep-herding dogs. One is the "heeler," who nips and barks at the heels of the sheep. The other type is a "header." Headers run ahead of the sheep and guide them. Border collies, such as Floss, are headers. Sheepdogs are trained to follow many commands and use several strategies to herd sheep in a desired direction.

- Why do you think dogs are good at herding sheep? Do you think another animal could do the job? What kind of animal? Why?
- What other types of animals besides sheep often need to be herded and kept in a group as they travel?
- How do you think a sheepdog is trained to do his or her job? How long do you think it takes to become a good sheepdog?

4. The people who look after sheep and move them from one pasture to another are called herders or shepherds. The shepherd directs the sheepdog by shouting or whistling commands. A shepherd's life can be a lonely one because there is not much companionship out in the countryside.

- Do you think the farmer in the story ever felt lonely? Why or why not?
- What do you do when you're feeling lonely?
- Would you like to be a shepherd? Why or why not?
- If you were a shepherd, what do you think your typical day would be like?

Extend Your Experience

Soccer

- soccer balls

Football, known as soccer in the United States, is Britain's most popular sport. Many children play the game at school and even Floss was an avid participant. Give children an opportunity to improve their coordination and ball-handling skills while practicing their best kicks, passes, and springs in the air just as Floss did.

Divide the class into groups of six players. Invite each group to form a circle and have students practice kicking the ball back and forth to one another. Remind students that they may not use their hands to control the ball. Depending on the level of your students, you might want to try a more challenging exercise, such as passing the ball (by kicking it) while players are running down a field. Encourage students to develop their own best moves just as Floss did and then demonstrate them for the class.

Making Scones

Though the traditional tea time associated with the British is no longer as widely observed as it once was, delicious tea-time treats are still enjoyed. Rich little tea cakes known as "scones" are very popular.

Scones	
• 2 cups (500 ml) flour	Sift together the flour, baking powder,
• 2 tsp (10 ml) baking powder	and salt. Cut in shortening. Add sugar
• ½ tsp (2.5 ml) salt	and currants and mix well. Stir in
• 4 Tbsp (60 ml) shortening	enough milk to form a stiff dough. Roll
• ¼ cup (60 ml) sugar	the dough to ¾" (2 cm) thick on a
• ¼ cup (60 ml) milk	lightly floured surface. Cut the dough
• ¼ cup (60 ml) currants	into 2-inch (5 cm) circles using the rim
(optional)	of a glass. (Or make mini-scones by
• butter and jam	cutting smaller circles.) Place the dough
	circles on a greased and floured cookie
	sheet and bake at 425°F (225°C) for
	about 10 minutes or until the tops are
	golden brown. Let the scones cool a bit,
	and then enjoy the warm scones with
	butter and jam.

Sheepdog Trials

- balloons
- cardboard
- rope

Floss worked hard to become a good sheepdog. The farmer took Floss to the dog trials to see how well she could compete with other well-trained sheepdogs. Give your students an opportunity to experience what Floss may have felt as they enjoy this game of "herding sheep."

Divide the class into equal teams to form relay lines. Place two balloons in front of each line. Using rope, outline a sheep pen at the opposite end of each relay line. Leave an opening in the sheep pen at the far side of the enclosure. The game begins with the first player from each team holding a cardboard flipper ("sheepdog"). The two balloons in front of each team are the "sheep." (Each team should have a different color of balloons.)

On the word "go," each player flips his or her sheep, one at a time, down the course and into the pen through the entrance. The player who gets two sheep in the pen first scores a point for the team. The sheep are positioned back at the starting line and the next player on each team takes a turn. The sheep may only be flipped with the cardboard and not touched in any other way. If a sheep is flipped into the pen any other way than through the entrance, it must be flipped out again and penned in the proper manner. The team that scores the most points after each member has had a turn is the winner.

Sheep in the Pasture

- butcher paper
- pastel chalk
- cotton balls
- construction paper
- scissors
- glue

Invite your students to recreate the soft portrait of rural life in England as depicted in the story. On a bulletin board or large sheet of butcher paper, use soft pastel colors to draw some softly rolling heather-covered hills. Invite students to make sheep using construction paper and cotton balls to add to the scene. Some students may want to make a soccer ball, draw children playing, and of course, add lively, playful, and hard-working Floss.

The Banza

Written by Diane Wolkstein and illustrated by Marc Brown
New York: Dial Books for Young Readers, 1981

Synopsis

In this Haitian story, Teegra and Cabree become the best of friends. As they part ways in the Haitian tropical forest, Teegra gives Cabree his family banza (banjo) and says it will provide protection. Before long, Cabree finds herself in serious trouble and discovers the special powers of the banza.

Background

Haiti is an island about 50 miles southeast of Cuba. This story was told to Diane Wolkstein while she was visiting Haiti. Marc Brown's illustrations incorporate some elements of basic Haitian art, such as bright colors, flat shapes, and varied patterns.

Deepen Your Understanding

1. Although the official language of Haiti is French, most people speak Haitian Creole, which is a mixture of French, Spanish, and African. Teegra (TEE▪gra) means "tiger" and Cabree (CAH▪bree) means "goat" in Creole.

    ▪ What were the names of the tiger and the goat? These names are from another language called "Creole." What language do you speak?

- Do you know any words from another language? What?
- Suppose you met a friend who spoke Creole., How could you talk to each other?

2. Use the example of this unlikely pair befriending each other to help children realize that even people who may be very different from each other can still share similarities.

- How were the tiger and the goat different?
- In what ways were the two alike?
- The tiger and the goat are usually considered enemies. What makes people enemies? Can enemies become friends? How?
- Is it possible to be friends with someone who is different from you? Why or why not?

3. Teegra gave Cabree a banza which belonged to his uncle. In Haiti, religious traditions were often passed down by uncles.

- What did Teegra give Cabree? Have you ever given something away that was very special to you? What?
- Have you ever received a special gift? What?
- What did Cabree do to show that the banza was important to her? How do you treat something that is important to you?

4. Some original folk songs in Haiti are actually chants and are performed according to the mood and feeling of the singer. The musical expression often combines African rhythms with French influences.

- Cabree expressed, in her song, what she hoped the tigers would believe to be her feelings of confidence, strength, and power. If you made up a song to tell others how you feel, what would the song be about?
- Cabree thought the banza made a friendly, happy sound. What kind of music makes you happy? Why?
- How did Cabree change the way the tigers felt about her and the way she felt about the tigers?
- Cabree was frightened in the beginning of the story. At the end she trotted off—for "her heart would have a new song." What do you think that means? Would you like to have a "new song" in your heart? Why? What frightens you?

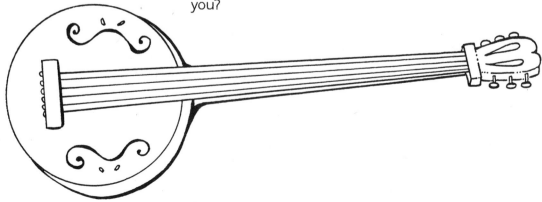

Extend Your Experience

Banza Tunes

- 7" (17.7 cm) paper plates
- crayons or markers
- scissors
- stapler
- rubberbands
- tagboard

The banza is a banjo that originated in Africa. It was made with a hollowed-out calabash gourd and hemp strings. Students can make a banza using two 7" (17.7 cm) paper plates and rubberbands. Give each child 2 paper plates. Invite students to first decorate the backsides of each paper plate using elements of Haitian art, such as bright colors, flat shapes, and varied patterns. Then help the children cut a 4" (10.2 cm) hole in the center of one of their plates. Staple the plates together (insides facing). The natural curve of the plates will create a hollow between them. Stretch rubberbands across the holes and add tagboard handles.

Palm Tree Art

- tagboard
- green construction paper
- scissors
- empty paper-towel rolls
- clay

Haiti has a wide variety of palm trees, including the royal palm that can grow as tall as 60 feet (18 m). Palm trees are a symbol of joy to Haitians. Invite children to point out the palm trees illustrated throughout the story. Make several 6" (15.3 cm) feather-shaped patterns from tagboard. Have each student trace a pattern several times on green construction paper to make palm fronds. Students can cut out the fronds, fold each in half lengthwise, and cut slits along the unfolded edge to add texture. Have children attach their fronds to one end of an empty paper-towel roll. Stick the other end of the rolls into clay bases to give the trees stability.

Island Hop

- drum

First, explain to the children that an island is completely surrounded by water and then invite students to locate Haiti on a map. To play "Island Hop," mark off three large "islands" on a play area. Number each island with a 1, 2, or 3. All players begin "swimming" in the "water" surrounding the islands, except one student. This student, with back turned to other players, beats a steady rhythm on a drum (Haiti's chief musical instrument). When the drum beats stop, each player chooses an island on which to rest. When all players are on an island, the drummer (still with back to other players) beats once, twice, or three times on the drum. All players resting on the island corresponding with the number of beats played are out of the game. Remaining players return to the water for a swim. Continue playing until only one player remains.

Haitian Storytellers

- *The Iguana's Tail* by Sir Philip Sherlock

In many cultures, the oral tradition of storytelling is how younger generations learn about the past. Tell children that the author of this book heard this story from a storyteller in Haiti. The storyteller began each story by shouting "Cric." Listeners eagerly replied "Crac" and the story began. Children may enjoy listening to some other "cric-crac" stories from *The Iguana's Tail* by Sir Philip Sherlock (see the bibliography on page 207). Invite children to tell the class a favorite story about themselves. Encourage children to say "Cric" and have their listeners reply "Crac" before beginning.

Nine-in-One Grr! Grr! A Folktale from the Hmong People of Laos

Told by Blia Xiong, adapted by Cathy Spagnoli, and illustrated by Nancy Hom
San Francisco: Children's Book Press, 1989

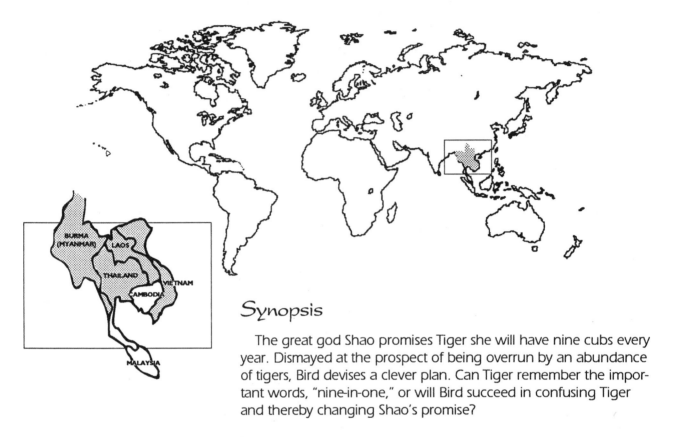

Synopsis

The great god Shao promises Tiger she will have nine cubs every year. Dismayed at the prospect of being overrun by an abundance of tigers, Bird devises a clever plan. Can Tiger remember the important words, "nine-in-one," or will Bird succeed in confusing Tiger and thereby changing Shao's promise?

Background

The Hmong (pronounced "Mong") come from the mountains of Laos, Thailand, Burma, and Vietnam. Blia Xiong first heard this story as a small child living in Laos. Cathy Spagnoli met Blia Xiong and at that time heard *Nine-in-One Grr! Grr!* for the first time. Both women are now working together to record more Hmong tales.

Deepen Your Understanding

1. In the story, Shao was kind and gentle and knew everything. He would not take back a promise and his words were absolute. In many Hmong villages, the oldest male member of the village is automatically the chief. What he says is respected by all.

   - Do you think Shao was wise to not break his promise?
   - Have you ever broken a promise?

- Who makes the decisions in your home?
- Whom do you go to for help to answer hard questions?
- Would you like to be the person others come to for advice and answers? Why or why not?

2. As illustrated in the story, the mountainous regions of Laos have tropical rain forests of broadleaf evergreens. There is an abundance of bamboo and wild banana trees. Encourage students to distinguish real from make-believe as they consider the environment and the story events.

- What are some things you saw in the story that you would probably not see on your way to school?
- If you had a chance to visit Laos, do you think you would see a tiger? Why or why not?
- Do you think it is true that there aren't many tigers today because Tiger could not correctly remember what Shao had told her?
- If you were telling about a trip that you took where you live, what are some things you would pass on your journey?

3. In Laos, families are very close and work together. Everyone in the family helps out, from the smallest child to the grandparents. Family ties are strong and often several generations will live together. In the story, Tiger wanted a family so she would not be lonely.

- What do you do when you are feeling lonely?
- What advice would you give to someone who told you they were lonely?
- Do you think everyone feels lonely sometimes? Why or why not?
- How does your family help you? How do you help your family?
- Do you think Tiger will be happy having only one cub each year?

4. The Hmong who live in the mountains have no roads or electricity. They carry their water from the nearest stream and grow most of their own food.

- Have you ever been camping and had to live without electricity? What was it like?
- Do you think living in the mountains would be difficult? Why?
- What would you grow, hunt, or gather if you couldn't buy your food in a store? How would you learn to do this?
- How do you think Hmong children feel when they come to live in this country? How would living here be different from living in the mountains in Laos?

Extend Your Experience

Fabric Fun

- felt or fabric scraps
- scissors
- glue
- dowels
- string

The illustrations in *Nine-in-One Grr! Grr!* were adapted from a technique of narrative stitchery known as a story cloth. These story cloths are the Hmong's unique way of recording their legends. Many Hmong women are expert seamstresses. They also make wall hangings by cutting and sewing bits of cloth. These wall hangings are called "pandau." The hangings may be geometric designs of diamonds, circles, or spirals repeated over and over. Invite children to notice the repetitive geometric borders around the illustrations in the story.

Have children work in small groups to recreate a favorite story using felt or fabric scraps. Each member in the group can design one scene from the story. (Or, students can make their own wall hangings.) Children can glue brightly colored fabric shapes on a banner. Fold the top of the banner over a thin dowel. Tie one end of a string to each end of the dowel to make a wall hanging.

Memory Chants

Tiger made up a little song so she would not forget Shao's promise. When parents ask their children to run an errand, they often use a memory chant to help them remember. For example, if a mother asks her son to go to a relative's house on the other side of the village to borrow an egg, she will teach the child a chant to help him remember why he is going.

Ask children whether or not they think they have a good memory. Ask them if they ever have trouble remembering what they have been told as Tiger did in the story. Help children recall some chants they have learned that help them remember important things (ABC song, "30 days has November . . ."). Invite children to recall something they have trouble remembering, such as a phone number or spelling a particular word. Encourage students to devise a chant that might help them remember the information.

Lots of Looks

- drawing paper
- crayons or markers

Usually, both Hmong men and women wear loose, blue or black pajama-type shirts and pants. Although in some Hmong subgroups, the women wear batik, pleated skirts, as illustrated on page seven in the story. The Hmong in Laos wear their own cotton cloth and dye it with indigo root to get a dark color. They then embroider the fabric. The women also wear embroidered head cloths like turbans.

Invite children to think about the clothing people wear in America. Specific clothing is worn by people in different occupations. Age is a factor in deciding on clothing styles, too. Your students probably do not wear the same style of clothing as their grandparents. Invite students to draw pictures of people wearing different or unique styles of clothing. Discuss the completed pictures and help students gain an appreciation for a variety of clothing styles.

Hmong Literature

Hmong literature contains elements common to many legends and tales, such as brave heroes, heroines in danger, and ferocious monsters. Most Hmong tales are not written, but told and handed down from parent to child. Point out some key elements of *Nine-in-One Grr! Grr!*, such as a character being tricked or fooled by another. Ask students to think of a story they have heard in which one character is fooled or tricked by another. For example, the Troll is tricked by the smallest Billy Goat in *The Three Billy Goats Gruff*. Invite students to work in groups to create an original story that uses this theme. Encourage groups to work cooperatively and then present their stories to the class.

Grandpa's Town

Written and illustrated by Takaaki Nomura
Translated by Amanda Mayer Stinchecum
New York: Kane/Miller Book Publishers, 1991

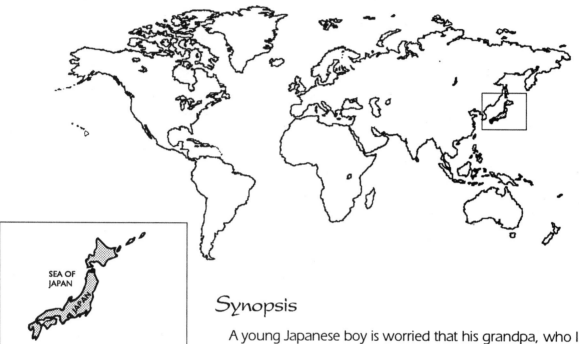

SEA OF
JAPAN

JAPAN

Synopsis

A young Japanese boy is worried that his grandpa, who lives alone, is lonely. He and his mother visit grandpa's town in hopes of persuading grandpa to come and live with them. But, after spending a day with his grandpa, Yuuta discovers his grandpa has many friends. (Text is in Japanese and English.)

Background

Japan, known as the Land of the Rising Sun, is an island country located off the coast of East Asia. It is made up of four main islands—Hokkaido, Honshu, Kyushu, and Shikoku.

Deepen Your Understanding

1. As Yuuta and his grandpa walked to the bath house, they passed many stores and stopped to talk to the fish man and the greengrocer. Invite children to look closely at the illustrations in the story and to compare and contrast the sights on the street in grandpa's town with the sights on a street in their neighborhood.

   - What are some of the places Yuuta and his grandpa stopped on their way to the bath house?
   - If you walked to a store near your home, what are some things you would pass along the way?

- What are some things you might see in Yuuta's neighborhood that you wouldn't see in yours?

2. Today, most Japanese families have their own bathrooms, but public bath houses are still popular as a place to meet and talk with friends. In fact, many bath houses have a second story with a tearoom and restaurant. Japan also has many hot springs and visiting them is a popular activity. Soap is never used in the bath itself. As depicted in the story, people soap and rinse themselves outside the bath and then get in to soak and relax.

   - How do you think Yuuta felt about going into the public bath house for the first time?
   - How would you have felt? Why?
   - Why do you think the people in Japan use public bath houses?
   - Where do you like to go to meet and talk with your friends?

3. As Yuuta and his grandpa left the bath house, the lady in the attendant's booth asked Yuuta to make a promise that he would come and visit again. She asked Yuuta to hook little fingers with her as a sign to seal the promise.

   - What do you do to seal a promise?
   - Do you think Yuuta will keep his promise? Why or why not?
   - Have you ever made a promise that you did not keep? Why?

4. Although Grandpa lived alone, he said that he didn't mind. Yuuta later realized that his grandpa had many friends and was not lonely. Encourage students to share times they have felt lonely and discuss how they feel when they are alone. Encourage students to be sensitive to people around them who may be lonely.

   - Do you think Grandpa ever felt lonely? Why or why not?
   - Have you ever felt lonely? When?
   - Do you like to be by yourself sometimes? When?
   - Do your grandparents live with you?
   - Do you think your grandparents are ever lonely?
   - What can you do to help someone who feels lonely?

Extend Your Experience

Japanese Characters

Point out the Japanese writing on each page of the story. Japanese is written in columns rather than across the page in rows. To read Japanese, you would start at the upper-right corner of a page, move down to the bottom, and then begin the next column to the left at the top of the page. Invite children to move their fingers across the English words showing the pattern their eyes would move if they were reading. Then, invite children to move their fingers across the Japanese words showing the direction they would read. Japanese is a difficult language to learn. It is a mixture of "kanji" and "kana" characters. Kanji are pictographs. Each symbol stands for a word or idea. Kanji characters cannot be sounded out. Either you recognize them or you don't. Kana characters each represent a syllable and can be sounded out. Invite children to learn how to say some Japanese words and phrases.

English	Japanese
good day	konnichi wa (koh•NEE•chee wa)
thanks	arígato (ar•ee•GAH•toe)
good-bye	sayonara (sigh•uh•NAR•uh)
teacher	sensei (SEN•say)

Getting to Know You

- lined paper
- pencil

By spending time in grandpa's town, Yuuta realized many things about his grandpa that he never knew. Most importantly, Yuuta realized that his grandpa was not lonely. Encourage children to get to know a grandparent or family member just as Yuuta did. Have each child think of a relative that they would like to know more about. Brainstorm a list of questions children would like to ask this person and write them on the chalkboard. Students can find out such things as who this family member's friends are, where he or she likes to go, or what he or she likes to do. Invite each child to prepare a list of questions using the ideas on the chalkboard. Children can ask the questions in person or write a letter to a family member they may have never met. Encourage children to introduce their family members to the class by sharing the information they have gathered.

Grocery List

- paper
- pencils

Many people in Japan go shopping every day. They buy food and household goods from neighborhood shops within walking distance. Because they buy daily from the same stores, they are known and valued as customers. Invite students to compare and contrast a grocery list Yuuta might make with one the class would make. As a class, compile a list of ten items students would be most likely to have on their shopping list if they were going to buy some food for their family. Write the list on the chalkboard. Then write the following list of items Yuuta and his grandpa might have on their grocery list.

chicken
milk
bread
mandarin oranges
eggplant
lotus roots
tofu
soy sauce
noodles
seaweed

Invite students to compare the two lists. Encourage students to write or dictate the items from Yuuta's list that they have never seen or tasted. Invite students to take the list with them the next time they go to the grocery store with their parents and try to find the items on the shelves. If possible, plan a field trip to an oriental grocery store.

Tatami Mats

- butcher paper
- scissors
- yardsticks or meter sticks
- pencils

Tatami mats are soft, springy mats that cover the floors of many Japanese homes. These mats are woven from rice straw and have a sweet, grassy smell when they are new. Most tatami mats are 6' x 3' (180 cm x 90 cm). Japanese room sizes are actually measured by the number of tatami mats it takes to cover the floor. An average room might have anywhere from four to eight tatami mats. Invite children to predict how many tatami mats it would take to cover the floor of their classroom. Record the predictions.

Then invite students to help measure and cut several 6' x 3' (180 cm x 90 cm) pieces of butcher paper. Have students use the pieces to measure the size of the classroom floor. Compare the actual results with the predictions. Then invite students to predict the tatami-size of a room in their home. Encourage children to take butcher paper "mats" home and test their predictions. Have students compare the size of a room, such as the living room or a bedroom, to the size of a room in a Japanese home.

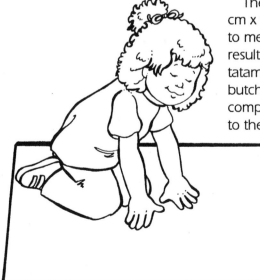

Tree of Cranes

Written and illustrated by Allen Say
Boston: Houghton Mifflin, 1991

SEA OF
JAPAN

JAPAN

Synopsis

A young boy in Japan celebrates his first Christmas as he learns the traditions of his mother's American childhood. The boy and his mother decorate a small tree with silver origami cranes and small twinkling candles. The next morning, the little boy finds a special gift under the tree.

Background

The traditional kimono, tatami mats, and wooden bath tubs are slowly disappearing from many Japanese homes in the name of convenience. The people of Japan have successfully combined what they consider to be the best of Japanese and Western ways of life. The author, Allen Say, was born in Yokohama, Japan.

Deepen Your Understanding

1. The little boy's mother was folding paper cranes in hopes that her wish would come true. In Japan, paper cranes are also given as a sign of best wishes. For example, paper cranes may be given to wish a sick friend better health or to wish someone good luck in a race or game. Invite students to brainstorm ways they have tried to ensure that a wish is granted (pulling on a wishbone, blowing out

birthday candles, or wishing on a falling star) or ways they send their friends best wishes (greeting card, small gifts).

- Why was the mother folding paper cranes?
- What do you do to make a wish come true?
- If you could have one big wish, what would you wish for?
- What do you do to let a sick friend know that you hope he or she feels better?
- How do you congratulate someone?

2. Bathing in Japan is often a form of relaxation. Some Japanese houses have a square, shoulder-deep wooden tub called an "o-furo." It is usually big enough for at least two people. It has a big lid that covers the water to keep it warm when no one is using it. People usually scrub clean before getting into the tub. Invite children to compare this tub to their own bathtub.

- How is the little boy's bathtub different from your bathtub?
- Have you ever sat in a tub similar to this one? When? What did it look like?
- Do you think it is relaxing to sit in a warm tub of water?
- What other ways do you like to relax?

3. Most Japanese now wear Western clothes, except for special occasions or relaxing at home. At home, Japanese adults might wear a "yukata," which is a long, loose cotton robe. It has flowing sleeves and is tied at the waist with a sash called an "obi." The mother in the story is wearing thick wooden sandals called "getas." Kimonos are often worn on special occasions, such as festivals and parties.

- What do you like to wear when you are relaxing around your home?
- Have you ever worn shoes that look like getas? What were they called?
- Do you ever wear special clothes for special occasions? What occasions? What do the clothes look like?

4. As depicted in the story, the typical interior of a Japanese home is simple in design. The straight, geometric patterns and sparsity of furniture are in harmony with the beauty of nature. The rooms have an air of purity and serenity. Nothing is overdecorated. A Japanese bed, like the little boy's bed in the story, is often a thin, cotton mattress called a "futon" laid on top of a tatami mat. Beds are often rolled up and stored out of sight during the day.

- How does the little boy's bedroom look different from your bedroom?
- If you were going to decorate a room, what would you put in it?
- What word would you use to describe your bedroom?
- What do you like about the little boy's bedroom? What do you think he might like about your bedroom?

Extend Your Experience

Origami Samurai Helmet

- newspaper

The little boy in the story wanted a samurai kite. When he woke up the next morning, he saw the fierce warrior staring at him from under the decorated tree. Samurai warriors are known for their strength and have long been the object of admiration for young Japanese. Invite your students to make a samurai helmet using the traditional art of Japanese paper-folding known as "origami."

Trim off the ends of large sheets of newspaper to make squares and give one to each child. Instruct children to fold point A down to point B. Fold corners C and D down to point B. Fold corners C and D up to point E. Fold points C and D outward. Fold the top sheet of point B upward. Fold the flap up again. Fold side corners behind. Fold the remaining flap behind. (An origami crane is a bit difficult for young children to make, but you might want to find the directions in an origami book and make one for the children to see as well.)

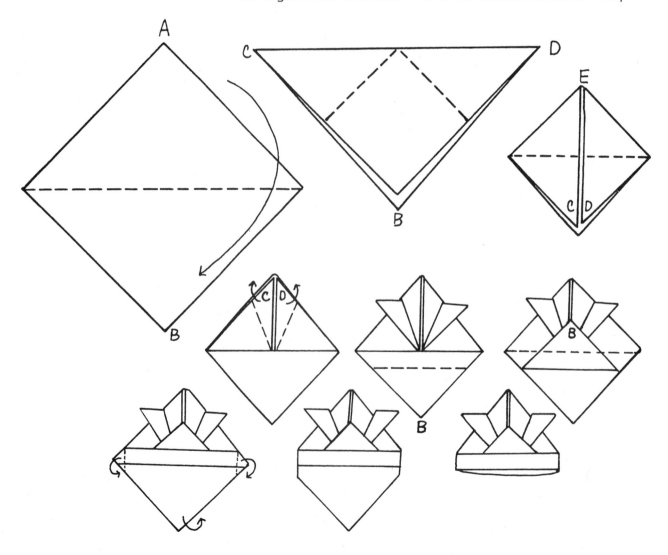

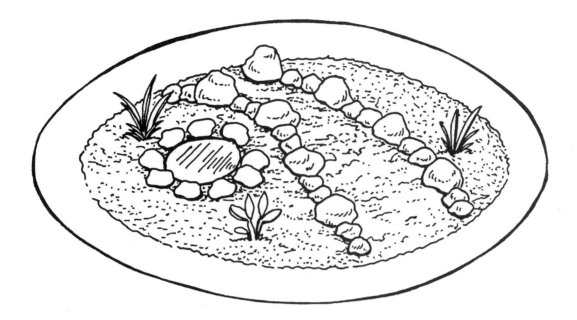

Bonkei

- paper plates or pie tins
- sand
- pebbles
- small plants

Because nature is an important theme in Japanese culture, wherever there is space, people make a garden. However, instead of lawns and flower beds, Japanese gardens contain pebbles, sand, rocks, trees, ponds, and running water. In many homes, a sliding door opens onto a carefully tended garden called a "tsuboniwa." "Bonkei" is the traditional art of making landscapes on a tray. Invite students to incorporate the themes of nature and simplicity as they make a tray garden.

Ask students to line a paper plate with a smooth layer of sand and add a few small pebbles, plants, or rocks in a simple, uncluttered arrangement. Students might want to add a small mirror to symbolize a pond or arrange some rocks in a stepping stone pattern. Invite students to create a one-, two-, or three-stone repeat pattern as the Japanese often do. For example, the pattern of two smaller stones followed by a larger one could be repeated over and over to make the desired path length.

Oshogatsu

- small slips of white paper
- pencils
- brown construction paper

Japan is a land of many festivals. The Japanese word for festival is "matsuri" and there are many matsuris throughout Japan. Invite your students to learn about a Japanese holiday, just as the little boy in the story learned about a holiday that his mother celebrated in California. The biggest celebration of the year is the New Year's festival called "Oshogatsu." One tradition of this holiday is to tie a fortune to a bare-branched tree to bring good luck.

Make a tree trunk using brown construction paper and display it on a bulletin board entitled "Bursting with Blossoms of Good Luck." Twist sheets of brown construction paper to make three-dimensional tree branches extending from the tree base. Invite each student to write or dictate a good luck wish or word of encouragement on a slip of white paper. Wishes might include such sentiments as "Hope you have a happy week!" "I'm glad you're my friend," or "Keep up the good work." Have students fold or crumple the fortunes and staple the "blossoms" on the tree. Choose one student each day to pick a blossom off the tree and read his or her good luck wish.

Kite Designs

- large plastic garbage bags
- tape
- string
- hole punch
- rags for kite tails
- 16" (40.8 cm) dowels

The boy in the story was excited to take his new kite outside. Kite flying is enjoyed all over Japan. A common reason for flying kites is to celebrate a happy event. Kites come in many shapes, with a variety of striking patterns or designs. Invite students to work in cooperative groups to create kites that will really fly. Give each group a piece of plastic garbage bag that has been cut to the following dimensions.

Have students tape a dowel from A to B and from C to D. Punch a hole at corner 1 and corner 2. Tie a 40" (102 cm) string through each hole. Tie both strings together and make a loop. Tie the flying string to this loop. Add three rag tails and invite groups to go outside and launch the kites.

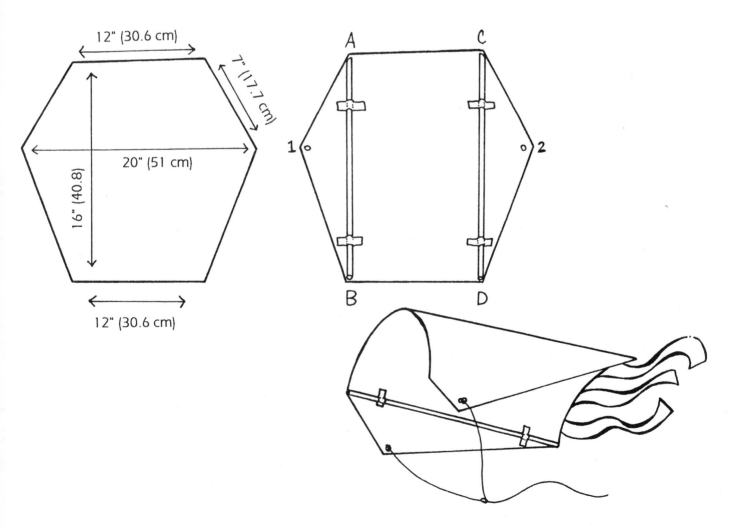

Llama and the Great Flood: A Folktale from Peru

Written and illustrated by Ellen Alexander
New York: Thomas Y. Crowell, 1989

Synopsis

Legend claims that high in the beautiful Andes mountains, many years ago, a llama had a dream. In this dream, a terrible flood destroyed the world. Knowing there was only one place that would be safe from the rising waters, the llama led his family to safety.

Background

The Andes are the most extensive range of mountains in the world. The North American Rockies are an extension of the same chain to which the Andes belong. This adaptation of an Andean myth tells what life might have been like for the native people known as the Inca. Inspired by her own travels in Peru, the author created this story to help children appreciate and understand this rich culture.

Deepen Your Understanding

1. Many cultures create folktales to explain nature. Among other things, this Peruvian folktale explains why the tip of the fox's tail is black. Also found in many cultures around the world is the story of a great flood. Encourage children to recall myths, folklore, and other stories that share these characteristics. Invite children to use their imaginations to create some tales of their own.

- How does the story of *Llama and the Great Flood* explain why the tip of the fox's tail is black?
- What are some other ways the tip of the fox's tail could have turned black?
- Do you know any other stories about a great flood?
- Imagine you are going to write a story about a great flood that happened right here where you live. Where would you go to be safe from the rising water? Who would you take with you?

2. The llama in the story carried supplies for the family up to the top of the mountain. Llamas can carry 100 pounds or more for distances of up to 20 miles a day. Although these beasts of burden still move goods through the Andes today, they are fast being replaced by trucks and trains. Discuss reasons why an animal may be a more efficient method of transportation in high mountainous country.

- If the family in the story had not had the llama to help them, how could they have carried their supplies up the mountain?
- How do community workers in your neighborhood move things from one place to another?
- Have you ever seen someone use an animal to help carry things? When?
- What are some other ways things can be moved from one place to another? Which way do you think is best? Why?

3. The llamas in the story wear ear tassels of dyed red yarn. This is a method of "branding" the animals for identification purposes. Red is a distinctive color of the Andeans. Because it looks different from any other red, it has been given the special name "rojo serrano."

- If you had a pet that was mixed up with a group of pets that looked alike, how would you know which one was yours?
- If your pet got lost and was found by someone else, how would they know it belonged to you?
- What ways are farm animals marked so the owners know who they belong to?

4. About one-third of Peruvians are highland farmers. People eat what they cultivate, which is most often maize (corn), potatoes, and beans. Meat is a luxury and usually smoked when eaten. Point out the illustration in the story that shows the mother and child packing food. Ask children to compare the family's "picnic" with the type of food they eat. Encourage children to discuss why the food is different.

- If you were going to pack a wonderful picnic, what food would you take?

- If you had to carry food for five days, what would you pack? Why?
- Where do you get the food you eat?
- What kind of food do you think the family in the story took with them?
- Where do you think the family got the food they ate?

Extend Your Experience

Is It Alive?

The illustrator of the story has attributed human characteristics to things we don't ordinarily consider living by giving the rocks and mountains in the story human faces. Encourage children to look for the faces in the illustrations as you read the story a second time. Then give children an opportunity to look for "humanness" in the nature around them. Find a grassy spot on a sunny day. Invite children to lie down and look up at the sky. As children study the cloud formations, encourage them to imagine shapes and faces. Students might also imagine faces in rocks and leaf shapes.

Weaving

- popsicle sticks
- brightly colored yarn
- glue

The woman on page 34 in the story is using a backstrap loom, which is one of many kinds of looms used by the Inca. The Inca are famous for their magnificent textiles. Another type of weaving that originated in Central and South America is done with a cross frame and many colors of yarn.

Give each student two popsicle sticks. Have children glue the two popsicle sticks together in the form of a cross. Allow the glue to dry thoroughly. Then invite children to wrap and weave various colors of yarn around and across the crossed sticks to create an interesting and colorful design.

Dried Foods

- fruits and vegetables and their dried by-products, such as:

  strawberry/strawberry fruit roll
  potato/dried potato product
  apple/dried apple chips
  grapes/raisins

The tool being used by the man on page 34 in the story is a digging tool used for planting potatoes. Potatoes were an important crop for the Incas. They dried the potatoes as a way of preserving them. The dried potatoes were called "chuño." To make chuño, the Incas spread the potatoes on the ground and left them overnight to freeze. The next morning they walked barefoot on them to squeeze out the water. They repeated the freezing and squeezing several times and then let the potatoes dry in the sun. These dried potatoes could be stored for several years. Discuss how the removal of water from a product is a way of preserving it.

Display the potato, apple, strawberry, and grapes and the dried products derived from them. Discuss the difference between the length of time each product will last. Invite students to bring in other dried foods to share with the class as well.

Pelea de Gallos

Pelea de Gallos is a traditional Peruvian children's game. Provide a six-foot (180 cm) diameter circle for each pair of players. (The game is best played on grass or mats.) Each player crouches with hands clasped under the knees and fingers intertwined in the position of a fighting rooster. In Peru, the players attempt to push their opponent out of the circle by jumping and bumping up against him or her. As each jump is made, the player must call out the name of a vegetable or animal product from the region. A player may not repeat something that has already been said. Modify the game to reinforce the cultural uniqueness of Peru. Instead of naming fruits or vegetables, invite students to name anything they remember from the story of *Llama and the Great Flood* or from your discussions that describe the culture. You might want to brainstorm a list of words before the game begins. Your list might include Inca, chuño, alpacas, llamas, Willka Qutu, potatoes, Andes, Peru, South America, and rojo serrano.

Tonight Is Carnaval

Written by Arthur Dorros and illustrated with arpilleras sewn
by the Club de Madres Virgen del Carmen of Lima, Peru
New York: Dutton, 1991

Synopsis

The excitement can hardly be contained as the countdown begins
for the arrival of Carnaval. Meanwhile, life goes on as usual with
much work to be done—preparing a field for planting, spinning
wool into yarn, and going to the market. But all the while, a young
Peruvian boy looks forward with great eagerness to playing his
"quena" in the band as the whole Carnaval sings and dances to his
music.

Background

This story takes place in the Andes mountains in the South American country of Peru. Arthur Dorros shared experiences similar to the
young boy's in the story when he visited Peru fourteen years ago.
After deciding to record his experiences in the form of a picturebook,
he met with a group of Peruvian women who agreed to sew the
illustrations. They used a native South American quilt art form known
as "arpilleras."

Deepen Your Understanding

1. Carnaval is the biggest festival of the year in Peru. It is held just
   before Lent, a period of fasting and repentance before Easter. As
   the story indicates, the music and dancing at Carnaval may go on

for several days. Encourage students to talk about celebrations they enjoy and compare their feelings of excitement with the young boy's feelings in the story.

- What did the young boy in the story do that showed he was anxious for Carnaval to begin?
- What celebrations do you look forward to?
- What are some ways you show your excitement?
- What is your favorite celebration? Why?
- In what ways are you like the young boy in the story?

2. There was much work to be done before Carnaval began. The family went about their usual chores. "Tunk, tunk, tunk" went Papa's axe as he chopped a log. "Pling, pling, pling" went the corn kernels as Mama boiled them in a pot. "Plonk, plonk, plonk" went the potatoes into the burlap bags. "Errr, errr, errr" went the coughing motor of the truck. Invite students to compare some of the Peruvian family's chores with their own.

- What are some chores you do around your home?
- Do you do any of the same chores that the boy in the story does? Why or why not?
- What is one chore that you do often? How would you describe the sound it makes?

3. Music was an important part of the young boy's life. He was not only looking forward to playing beautiful music for Carnaval, but he also enjoyed music as he went about his everyday chores. He made up songs about mountains and friends. He also played a song on his "quena" about llamas called "Mis Llamitas."

- Have you ever made up a song? What was it about?
- The young boy made up songs about llamas, mountains, and friends. What would you like to write a song about? Why?
- If the young boy were going to write words to go with his music, what do you think he might say about the llamas?

4. The family in the story grew many kinds of potatoes. Potatoes, as well as other foods, such as corn, beans, gourds, chiles, cocoa, and tomatoes, were first grown and cultivated in North and South America. We often think of rich tomato sauce as Italian. We call fried potatoes "French" fries. And, many fine chocolates are associated with the Swiss. However, these foods were all unknown to the Europeans until they sailed to the Americas. Invite students to think of foods that contain these ingredients that they enjoy eating.

- What type of potatoes do you enjoy eating?
- Have you ever eaten any of these other foods that were first grown in the Americas? Which ones?
- Have you ever eaten any dishes that were made from these foods? What?

- What is your favorite food?
- Do you know where it was first grown?

Extend Your Experience

Camel Family

- construction paper (brown and white)
- scissors
- glue
- cotton balls
- crayons or markers

In the story, the little boy takes his llamas high in the mountains to find grass to eat. He also carries wool from an alpaca to his mother so she can spin it into yarn. Ninety percent of all members of the camel family live in the highlands of Peru or Bolivia. The llama is considered a beast of burden and can carry heavy loads for many miles. The alpaca is primarily a producer of wool. White alpaca wool (as depicted in the story) is most valuable because it can be dyed any color. But the animals' fur is also brown, gray, and black.

Invite the children to make a llama or alpaca from construction paper. Give each child a sheet of brown construction paper. Help the children round the top edges so the papers take on the shapes of a tall Andes mountain. Invite children to each draw an alpaca and a llama on white construction paper and cut them out. Have children glue both animals on the brown mountain. So children can remember the purpose of each camel family member, invite children to cover the alpacas with wool (cotton balls) and glue small bundles on the camels' backs.

Carnaval Sounds

- recorders
- balloons
- coffee cans
- oatmeal containers
- heavy string
- popsicle sticks
- copper tubing or sprinkler pipe
- tape

Music is an important part of Carnaval and it was particularly important to the young boy in the story. Review the pictures and descriptions of the musical instruments in *Tonight Is Carnaval*. Encourage students to create or use musical instruments with similar characteristics in their own sound symphony. A recorder is similar to a flute and can be played as a quena. Students can make a bombo by stretching a balloon over the open end of a small coffee can. Or, cut a round oatmeal container in half and tape the sides together so that the sealed ends face upward. This makes a great bongo drum. Students can make a bass fiddle by threading a heavy string through a hole in the bottom of a coffee can. Tie a knot in the string so it won't pull back through the hole. Tie the remaining end to a popsicle stick and pull the string taut. With one foot on the can and one hand holding the string taut, students can use their free hand to pluck the string. To make a zampoña, try taping different lengths of copper tubing or sprinkler pipe together. When the instruments are complete, invite some children to create Carnaval sounds while others dance in a long, winding line.

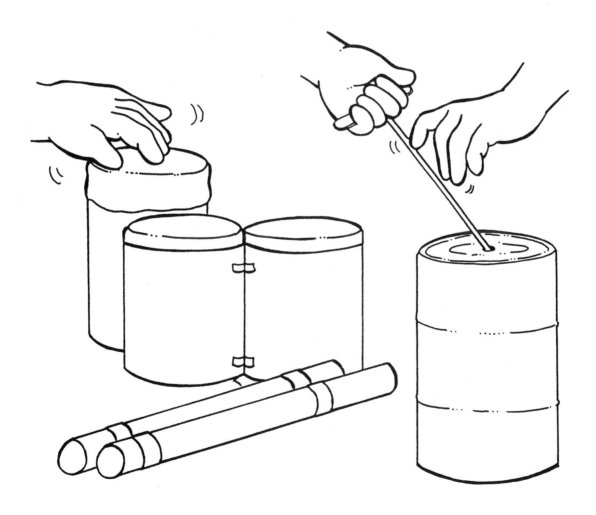

Arpilleras

- construction paper
- tissue paper or cotton balls
- glue
- crayons or markers

It is often said that a picture is worth a thousand words. This seems to be true as evidenced by the beautiful hand-stitched "arpilleras" in the story. These traditional wall hangings are made from cut and sewn pieces of cloth. They tell stories of important events in everyday life. They often have pockets on the back to hold a written copy of the story pictured. Give children an opportunity to make intricate patchwork pictures that tell stories about themselves. Children can glue brightly colored construction paper pieces on a background. Stuff a piece of tissue or cotton behind some of the pieces to give them a three-dimensional effect. Invite older children to use felt or fabric and a needle and thread to create a tapestry. Help children make pockets for the backs of their arpilleras. Encourage students to write or dictate stories to add to the pockets.

Potato Harvest

- potato
- box of dried potatoes
- lined paper
- pencils

Notice the arpilleras that show the variety of potatoes growing beneath the ground. Potatoes are a very important part of the diet of the Andeans. In fact, potatoes were first farmed in the Andes mountains of South America. The Inca have been credited for being the first to develop a method for freeze-drying potatoes.

Display a potato and a box of dried potatoes. Ask students how the two are the same and how they are different. Invite students to describe or bring in a recipe of their favorite way to eat potatoes. Compile the potato recipes into a class book of tasty treats. Set aside a day for a "potato harvest" by inviting parent volunteers to help the students prepare and enjoy some of the potato treats.

Yagua Days

Written by Cruz Martel and illustrated by Jerry Pinkney
New York: Dial Books for Young Readers, 1976

Synopsis

Adan thought that rainy days were terrible days in New York's Lower East Side. Instead of playing in the park, he could only watch the cars splash by on the street. But after Adan's visit to Puerto Rico, he discovers the belly-flopping fun of the wet and wonderful yagua days.

Background

Puerto Rico is an island in the Caribbean just east of Haiti and the Dominican Republic. The capital city of the island was originally named Puerto Rico ("rich port") because of its well-protected harbor. Possibly through a mapmaker's misunderstanding, the name of the island and the harbor were switched. The capital city became known as San Juan and the island became Puerto Rico.

Deepen Your Understanding

1. Adan experienced many emotions common to children all over the world. Point out these similarities and shared feelings.

   - Adan would much rather be playing in the park than helping his father in the bodega. Are there times when you would rather be doing something else? When?

- Adan had a "long face" because it was raining. What is a long face? What gives you a long face?
- Adan found out how he could turn his long-face days into fun days. How could you turn your long-face days into fun days?

2. Jorge teased Adan by telling him the fruit and vegetables he delivered in New York actually grew in his truck. But, while in Puerto Rico, Adan learned that the produce his father sold in the bodega is grown on a finca. He learned that mangoes and oranges come from trees. Gandules come from bushes and ñames are grown under the ground.

- Have you ever seen ñames, gandules, or mangoes in a store where you live?
- What are some foods that grow on trees that you have seen in your store?
- What are some foods that grow under the ground that you have seen before?

3. Puerto Rico's climate is mildly tropical. Temperatures average 70° F (21°C) to 80° F (27° C) year round. The island averages 65 inches (166 cm) of rain each year reaching nearly 200 inches (5 m) annually in the rain forest. Compare the climate and seasonal activities where you live with that of Puerto Rico.

- Adan realized that there were some things he could not do when it rained and some things he could only do when it rained. What are some things you cannot do when it rains?
- Is there anything you can do only if it rains? What?
- Have you ever gone sliding down a snowy mountain on a sled or gone down a water slide? What type of weather do you need for these activities?
- Notice the clothing Adan and his family wore in the story. Were any of them wearing a coat or mittens? Why not?
- Do you ever need to wear warm clothing where you live? When? What is the weather like now where you live?

4. While Puerto Ricans speak Spanish, many of them are also fluent in English. Spanish is the language of instruction in the schools, but English is taught as a second language. Point out the Spanish words and their meanings used throughout the story. Compare and contrast the Spanish words with some English equivalents.

- Adan stood in the doorway of his parents' bodega. What is a bodega? What word means about the same thing in English?
- Jorge greeted Adan by saying, "Qué pasa." What greeting do you use when you see a friend?
- When Jorge left the bodega, he said "Hasta luego." What do you say to your friends when you are leaving?

Extend Your Experience

Tree Frogs

- clay
- tempera paint
- paintbrushes

Coquies (koh-KEES) are small tree frogs found almost nowhere else but in Puerto Rico. They are considered Puerto Rico's national symbol. Although the frog is only about 1 1/2 inches (3.8 cm) in size, its nocturnal voice is very powerful. The frog was named after its two-note song, "ko-kee." Throughout the island the coqui can be heard "singing" from sunset to dawn. But in the rain forest, the birdlike chirps can be heard day and night. Remind students that Adan woke one morning to the sound of these tree frogs beeping like tiny car horns. Invite students to make small (1 1/2" or 3.8 cm) frogs from clay. After the clay has hardened, encourage students to paint and add details to the frogs. Help children realize the environmental differences between Puerto Rico and where they live.

Making Tostones

Foods in Puerto Rico come from a variety of ethnic backgrounds, including Spanish, Indian, and African. Adan and his family enjoyed sitting under wide trees and eating arroz con gandules, pernil, viandas and tostones, ensaladas de chayotes y tomates, and pasteles. Ask students what foods they enjoy eating with their families. Give students an opportunity to taste fried platanos, known as tostones (tohs•TONE•ays). Platanos are green bananas that must be cooked to be eaten.

Tostones	
• platanos	Peel and slice platanos into one-inch (2.5 cm) thick
• oil	rounds. Fry in oil until soft and slightly brown. Drain
• paper towels	on paper towels. Flatten the platanos with a mallet
• salt	and fry again until crisp. Drain on paper towels.
	Season with salt and enjoy. Tostones are often
	served the way French fries are served in the
	United States.

Bolsa de Fruta

- tropical fruit, fruit juices, or pictures of tropical fruit (optional)

Spanish is the official language of Puerto Rico, but English is widely spoken and a required subject in school. This activity will give children a chance to practice Spanish words as well as become more familiar with tropical fruits common to the Puerto Rican islanders. If possible, show a sample of each tropical fruit mentioned in the story or show pictures. If tropical fruits are not available, there are many tropical fruit juices children may like to sample.

Play a version of "Fruit Basket Upset." Have children sit in chairs in a circle with one player standing in the middle. Assign each child the name of tropical fruit mentioned in the story (mango, quenepa, mapenes, coconut, guanábana). The standing player calls out the name of one fruit. All players with that name must exchange places. The standing player tries to sit in one of the empty chairs leaving a new player standing in the middle. At any time, the standing player may also call out "Bolsa de Fruta" (bowl-sa day fruit-ah), in which case every player must find a new seat.

Large Leaves

- fallen leaves
- butcher paper
- pencils
- scissors

Uncle Ulise picked up the yagua from the wet grass. It had fallen from a palm tree. Fallen leaves from the "yagrumo" tree are everywhere in the forests of Puerto Rico. Invite students to gather leaves that have fallen to the ground where they live. Encourage students to estimate the size of the yagua by noticing its size in comparison to Adan. Invite students to cut out a giant leaf from butcher paper about the size they think a yagua is. Have students estimate how many of their collected leaves it would take to equal the size of one yagua. After making a prediction, invite students to cover the butcher-paper yagua with leaves to test their estimate. As a homework assignment, have a contest to see who can find the largest leaf to bring into class. Remind students not to pick leaves from a tree, but only to gather fallen leaves.

The Great Kapok Tree: A Tale of the Amazon Rain Forest

Written and illustrated by Lynne Cherry
New York: Harcourt Brace Jovanovich, 1990

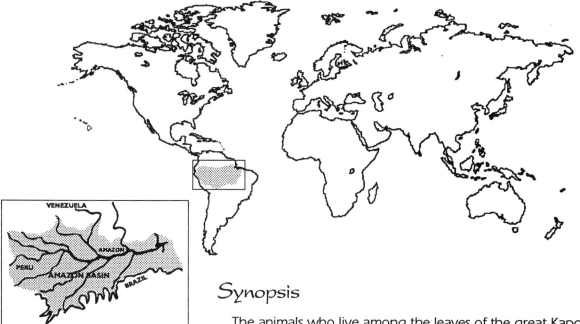

Synopsis

The animals who live among the leaves of the great Kapok tree in the Amazon rain forest watch in silence as a man begins to chop down their home. After much chopping, the tired man rests at the foot of the huge tree where he soon falls asleep. One by one, the animals whisper in the man's ear begging him not to destroy their home.

Background

The Amazon Basin in South America contains the largest rain forest in the world. The rain forest spreads out over the countries of Brazil, Ecuador, Colombia, and Venezuela. It is home to hundreds of thousands of species of plants, animals, and insects. Lynne Cherry traveled to the Amazon rain forest in South America in preparation for writing and illustrating this beautiful book.

Deepen Your Understanding

1. Most rain forests are "tropical rain forests." They are near the equator where the weather is warm all year long. In addition to the warm temperature, several inches of rain can fall in just one hour. Rain forests have been known to get up to 30 feet (9 m) of rain in one year. Because of the large amounts of precipitation,

the forest stays green all year. Discuss the climate similarities and differences between the rain forest and where your students live.

- What is the weather like where you live?
- Why do you think the rain forest is so green?
- Can you think of a place that gets very little rain? What does it look like?
- How is the rain forest different from where you live? How is it the same?
- What are some kinds of clothes you would not need to pack in your suitcase if you were going to visit the Amazon rain forest? What clothes should you bring if you were visiting the rain forest?

2. The animals were concerned that their home in the rain forest was being destroyed. Help children understand that taking something for ourselves often means that we are taking away from someone else. Encourage children to see how they can protect and care for their own natural environment.

- Why would a man want to chop down a tree?
- What would the chopped-down tree be used for?
- What happens when trees are cut down in your community?
- Why is it important to plant new trees?
- How can you help save trees?

3. *The Great Kapok Tree* is dedicated to Chico Mendes. He was a very brave man who dedicated his life to saving the Amazon. His full name was Francisco "Chico" Mendes Filho.

- Chico Mendes believed very strongly in saving the rain forest. Is there anything that you believe very strongly in? What? Why?
- What could you do to let other people know how you feel?
- Many people disagreed with Chico Mendes, but it did not change the way he felt. How do you feel when someone disagrees with something you think is very important? Do you change your mind?

4. The Yanomamo tribe is the largest group of Amazonian forest people. They fall into the category of Tropical Forest Indians called "foot people." Their daily life is constructed around taking care of their own needs and the needs of the forest. The Yanomamo believe that the forest will always look after them if they respect it.

- How do you think the forest can look after or take care of the people who live there?
- What do you think the Yanomamo do to take care of the forest?
- How does your environment (trees, plants, rain) take care of you?
- How do you take care of your environment?

Extend Your Experience

Save a Tree

- Rainforest Crunch ice cream or nut brittle
- construction paper
- crayons or markers

An area of rain forest is being destroyed every minute. If the destruction continues at this rate, there may be no rain forests left in the future. But there are people all over the world who are working to save these valuable forests. Although we use thousands of kinds of plants for food and medicine, there are ways to use the products without destroying the rain forest. For example, nuts are collected from the forest without harming it. Give students a chance to sample Rainforest Crunch nut brittle or a flavor of Ben & Jerry's ice cream called "Rainforest Crunch." A portion of the profits from such products are donated to salvation efforts.

Then invite children to design "Save a Tree" posters. Encourage children to create slogans using some of the messages that the animals whispered in the man's ear. For example, the bee contended that all living things depend on one another. The porcupines pointed out that trees produce oxygen. And, the sloth emphasized that without the beauty of the luscious green forest there would be nothing upon which to feast your eyes. Help the children write the slogans on the bottoms of pieces of construction paper. Then invite children to illustrate their "Save a Tree" posters.

Layers of Life

There are many layers of life in the Amazon rain forest. Each layer provides a different kind of home to the animals that live there. The top layer of trees is called the "canopy." Some animals spend their entire lives in the canopy and never touch the ground. Trees in the canopy can grow to be over 100 feet (30 meters) tall. Extremely tall trees, such as the Kapok tree, can shoot up beyond the canopy. The "understory" is the layer of smaller trees and plants that grow below the canopy. The animals in the understory live in a dark and shadowy environment. The lowest layer is the "forest floor." Draw a diagram on the chalkboard showing the layers of life in the rain forest. Read The Great Kapok Tree again and make a list on the chalkboard of all the animals mentioned in the story. Ask children to listen closely to find out where each animal lives. Record the animal names in the appropriate place on the layer diagram.

Rain Forest Mural

- butcher paper
- green fingerpaint
- yellow and black paint
- collage materials, such as tissue paper, toothpicks, construction paper, and sponges

The Amazon rain forest, as so beautifully illustrated by Lynne Cherry, is a lusciously green paradise that is rich with life. Divide the class into small groups of four to six to create rain forest murals. Give each group a large sheet of butcher paper on which to fingerpaint a green background. Encourage children to use their fingers, sides of their hands, and palms to create interestingly textured foliage. While the backgrounds are drying, invite children to create three-dimensional plants and animals. Make butterflies from brightly colored tissue paper, create porcupines using toothpicks, and design a jaguar's dappled coat with yellow and black sponge paint. Attach plants and animals to the dried background to complete the rain forest community.

Animals of the Rain Forest

- resource books on rain forest animals
- construction paper
- crayons or markers

In the rain forest, you can find more kinds of plants and animals than anywhere else on earth. Scientists believe that for every kind of plant or animal that we know of there are over 20 yet in the rain forest to learn about. Give children an opportunity to learn some interesting facts about the animals mentioned in the story. Divide the class into cooperative groups. Assign each group an animal from the story (toucan, macaw, cock-of-the-rock, tree frog, jaguar, porcupine, anteater, sloth) and ask students to make a large picture of their assigned animals. Provide resource books with pictures for the students to use. Display the pictures on a bulletin board entitled "Did You Know . . ." Share some interesting facts about the animals and print the facts on cards to display next to the pictures.

A tree frog can leap in the air to catch insects that are coming its way.

A toucan will eat small fruits and berries whole and maybe a spider for dessert.

An anteater can walk on its knuckles and has a tongue 8 to 10 inches (20.4 to 25 cm) long.

A cock-of-the-rock can spread its feathers out so they look like a shawl.

Atariba & Niguayona

Adapted by Harriet Rohmer & Jesus Guerrero Rea and illustrated by Consuelo Méndez
San Francisco: Children's Book Press, 1987

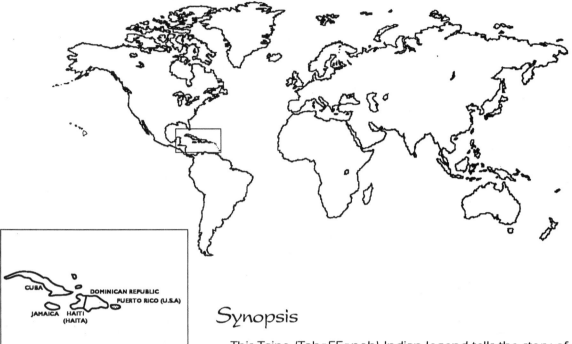

Synopsis

This Taino (Tah•EE•noh) Indian legend tells the story of a young boy's search for the healing caimoni tree. Niguayona begins his search while his very sick friend lies in a hammock in the village healer's hut. Despite fatigue, discouragement, and hunger, Niguayona perseveres to become a true hero. (Text in Spanish and English.)

Background

The Taino, an Arawak people, lived in Puerto Rico at the time of the Spanish conquest. Puerto Rico is one of several islands in the Caribbean Sea. It is significant that in this story, a tree is able to save the life of a friend, for the Taino were agricultural people. They cultivated potatoes, cassava, peanuts, peppers, and beans.

Deepen Your Understanding

1. As depicted in the story, body paint was common among the Taino people. A yellow-orange paint was often made from achiote berries, which are seeds from the annatto tree. Achiote is used today in Puerto Rico to color and flavor food. People of all cultures like to adorn their bodies in ways they find attractive.

Because of the hot climate in the Caribbean, most people do not wear much clothing. Instead of clothing, the Taino made their bodies look attractive by painting them and wearing jewelry. Discuss some of the reasons why your students dress differently from the way Atariba and Niguayona dressed.

- Why do you think the Taino painted their faces and bodies?
- What do you like to wear to make yourself look your very best?
- In what ways do Atariba and Niguayona look different from you?
- In what ways are they the same?

2. After discussing some of the differences between the Taino people and your students, point out similarities as you discuss the story characters' friendship. Niguayona enjoyed walking along the riverbank, playing, and making things with his friend. Niguayona cared so much for Atariba that he was willing to do anything he could to save her.

- What do you enjoy doing with your friends?
- Niguayona missed walking along the riverbank with his friend. What would you miss most about one of your friends if you could no longer spend time with him or her?
- Would you have gone to as much trouble to save one of your friends as Niguayona did to save Atariba? Why?
- In what ways are you like Niguayona?

3. Notice the picture on page two of Atariba sleeping in a hammock. The name for this space-saving type of bed comes from the Taino word "hamaca." Explain to students that a hammock is a hanging bed often made from netting or canvas. Each end of the bed has a cord or rope that is tied to a special support. Hammocks are popular today in many tropical countries around the world for sleeping and lounging. Encourage children to see that the natives of a land make significant and lasting contributions to the lifestyles of those who follow.

- How is the bed Atariba is sleeping in different from yours?
- Have you ever rested in a hammock? Would you like to? Why or why not?
- If you were going to design a bed, what would it look like?

4. The bohique (boh-EE-keh) was the village healer. He often used herbs and plants as medicine. The bohique also asked advice from the spirits to help diagnose the patient's condition and to decide on a cure. Help students compare the village healer to a doctor in their community.

- If you had a friend who was sick, who would you ask for help to make your friend feel better?
- The Taino called the village healer a "bohique." What do you call the person who helps sick people where you live?
- What are some things that are the same or different about a bohique and a doctor?
- Why do you think the bohique could not heal Atariba?

Extend Your Experience

Friendship Necklace

- string or yarn
- colored macaroni, fruit-flavored cereal rings, or clay and paint

The Taino people were advanced in their intricate carvings in stone, wood, clay, and shellwork. In the story, Niguayona made a beautiful necklace of sea shells and green stones for his friend. A major theme throughout the story is that of friendship. Encourage students to make a special necklace as a sign of friendship for a classmate, playmate, or family member.

Provide students with a variety of materials to thread on a piece of string or yarn. Students can make necklaces by stringing colored macaroni or colored fruit-flavored cereal rings. Students can also make beads from clay. After the clay dries and hardens, children can paint the beads. Encourage students to make their necklaces unique and then present them to their special friends.

Taino Taste Treats

- cassava, known as "yuca"
- anon or custard apple

The food staple of the Taino tribe was the cassava. It is a root vegetable of a leafy shrub native to South America. You can find cassava in many Hispanic markets under the name "yuca." Peel the dark, rough, bark from the vegetable and boil it until it is soft. Make a "mojo" (savory sauce or dressing) by sautéing garlic, onion, sour orange, and lime in olive oil. Pour the mojo over the hot yuca. Enjoy!

The anona fruit mentioned in the story is known as an "anon" in Hispanic markets. It is also called "custard apple." It has a sweet, creamy, white flesh and is fun to eat because you have to suck the fruit off the large, black pits. Two or three anons would be enough for your students to each have a small sample.

Nature Appreciation

- construction paper
- crayons or markers

Nature is highly respected in the Taino culture. The bold illustrations in the story as well as the significance of plants and animals in Niguayona's quest portray nature's importance. Ask children to recall ways in which nature helped Niguayona along his journey. For example, a macaw whispered in Niguayona's ear, the anona lit the way, the river carried Niguayona, and the red fruit from the caimoni tree healed Atariba. The Taino believed that Niguayona was successful because he listened to the natural forces around him. Encourage children to take a closer look at the nature that surrounds them. Invite each student to make a poster illustrating one part of their natural environment. Encourage students to celebrate and appreciate its importance just as the Taino did. Invite children to share their poster with the class and tell why nature is important to them. For example, a student might recognize that a tree provides shade on a hot day, the sun brings warmth, or fruit is a tasty snack.

Musical Celebration

- plastic eggs
- rice or beans
- masking tape

After Atariba recovered, the Taino people celebrated with songs and dances. Ask students what type of music and dancing they think might have been included in the fiesta. Music is a rich form of artistic expression in Puerto Rico. The Taino often danced to the accompaniment of gourd rattles called "maracas." Invite students to make maracas by filling large plastic eggs with rice or beans. Seal the eggs tightly and wrap the seams with tape if necessary. Students can shake their maracas in unison or in groups to create some interesting rhythms.

Rechenka's Eggs

Written and illustrated by Patricia Polacco
New York: Philomel Books, 1988

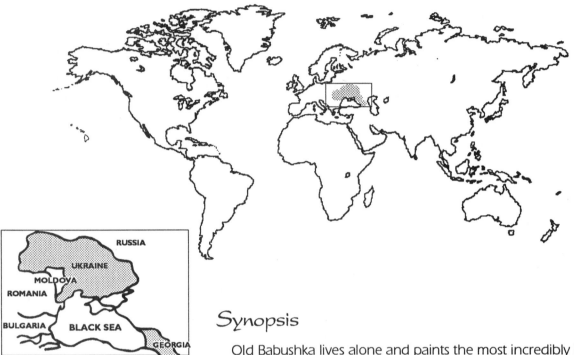

Synopsis

Old Babushka lives alone and paints the most incredibly beautiful eggs. Babushka becomes quite fond of a wounded goose she has taken in. One day the goose accidentally breaks the lovely hand-painted eggs. But the miracle that awaits Babushka the next morning is the first of many to follow.

Background

The Ukraine, which is a former province of Russia, is located in southeastern Europe along the Black Sea. Patricia Polacco's family roots lead back to the countries of the Ukraine and Georgia. She shares Babushka's love of painting intricately beautiful Ukrainian eggs in her spare time.

Deepen Your Understanding

1. Babushka considered it a miracle that herds of wild caribou had found their way to her. She also thought a miracle had replaced the broken eggs with even more beautiful eggs. And, Babushka considered the gift Rechenka left her a miracle as well.

   - Why do you think Babushka considered all of these events miracles?
   - Do you think they were miracles?

- What is a miracle?
- Do you think this story is real or make-believe? Why?
- What kind of miracle would you like to happen to you?
- Do you think the little goose Rechenka left for Babushka was able to lay painted eggs? Why or why not?

2. Babushka took great pride in her work. She was known far and wide for her delicately hand-painted eggs and she always won first prize at the Easter Festival in Moskva. Encourage children to see the value in working carefully and doing their best.

- Why do you think Babushka works so carefully on her eggs? How would the eggs be different if she had rushed to finish them?
- Do you do your work as carefully as Babushka did? How are you similar to Babushka? How are you different?
- What does it mean to take pride in your work? What can you do that you feel proud of?
- How do you think Babushka feels when she wins first prize every year? Have you ever won a prize? How did you feel?

3. The festival in this story is a combination of the Russian Orthodox Easter processional worship and food blessing and the old-fashioned village springtime celebration. After the drab, cold winter, villagers put on bright clothes and sell food, entertain each other, and have contests. This festival includes special foods, like kulich, pashka, and brightly painted eggs. These symbolize the renewing of the earth that takes place in the spring. Other spring festivals include the Cherry Blossom Festival, Purim, and May Day.

- What spring holidays do you celebrate?
- How are your celebrations like the one in the story? How are they different?
- What do many spring celebrations have in common? Why do you think this is so?
- Have you ever been to a spring festival? What did you like about it?

4. In the story, Babushka cares for and about animals. She feeds grasses to the caribou in winter, nurses Rechenka back to health, and enjoys the sight of newborn caribou calves. In the end, she is left with a "miraculous" baby goose. Encourage children to examine relationships between animals and humans.

- In what ways do you think Babushka's life changed after she took care of Rechenka? In what ways do you think Rechenka's life changed after she was rescued by Babushka?
- Do you have a pet? How is your life and the life of your pet different now that you have each other?
- Why do you think Babushka let Rechenka go free? What would you have done? Why?
- What made the little goose extra special for Babushka? Why didn't she set it free, too?

Extend Your Experience

Pysanka

- hard-boiled eggs
- tempera paint in small containers
- cotton swabs
- cardboard tubes

Ukrainians are famous for their craft of decorating eggs called "pysanky." The intricately created designs and symbols painted on the eggs have meaning and significance. For example, waves and ribbons symbolize life without end. Colors have significance, too. Red symbolizes love, pink is for success, and blue for health. Children in the Ukraine enjoy learning to decorate these eggs. It is an art that takes practice and skill. Invite your students to practice the art of pysanky. Give each child an egg and place the paint and cotton swabs within easy reach. Invite children to dip the cotton swabs into the various colors and paint designs and patterns on their eggs. A ring cut from a cardboard tube makes a perfect egg stand.

Babushka's Dacha

Remind students that most people who live in the Ukraine do not speak English. Review some of the words Babushka used in the story. Play a variation of "Red Light, Green Light" in which everyone tries to get into Babushka's dacha (house). Choose one child to be Babushka. Then have all the other students line up facing Babushka at the other end of the room or field. Babushka stands in a designated spot and says "Da" each time she turns away from the students. Students run forward until Babushka turns back and says "Niet," at which time the children must freeze. Any player who moves during a freeze may be sent back to the start. The first child to reach Babushka's dacha and tag her is the next Babushka.

Making Kulich

Babushka and Rechenka enjoyed eating a special Easter bread known as "kulich." Make and share this delicious coffee cake with your students.

Kulich	1
• 2 pkgs yeast	Dissolve the yeast in milk. Add 1
• 1 cup (250 ml) milk (lukewarm)	cup (250 ml) flour and mix. Let
• 5 cups (1 ¼ l) flour	the dough rise in a warm place for
• ½ lb (225 ml) butter	about one hour. Cream butter and
• 1 ½ cups (375 ml) sugar	gradually add sugar, beating until
• 10 egg yolks	light and creamy. Add the egg
• ½ cup (125 ml) each of candied	yolks one at a time. Then add this
fruit, toasted slivered	mixture to the risen dough. Add
almonds, and raisins	the rest of the flour and knead
• two 2-lb (900 ml) coffee cans	the dough until it is smooth and
• waxed paper	elastic. Add more flour, if neces-
	sary. Place the dough in a greased
	bowl, cover, and let rise about one
	hour. Then punch the dough down

	2

and add fruit, almonds, and raisins.
Butter the two coffee cans and line them with buttered waxed paper.
Allow the waxed paper to extend over the top. Place the dough in the
cans and let the dough rise until doubled and almost to the top. Bake
at 350°F (180°C) for 45 to 60 minutes. The cake will mushroom over
the top. Remove the bread from the cans and cool. To serve, cut
horizontal slices from the top. The first slice is saved and used as a
lid for the cake.

Old Moskva

- sponges cut into geometric shapes (squares, triangles, arches, onion domes)
- tempera paint
- construction paper
- markers or crayons

Invite students to notice the onion domes of Old Moskva as illustrated in the story. Onion domes have been used to decorate Russian Orthodox churches since the mid-1500s. Invite students to make sponge-painted pictures depicting these distinctive domes. Students can "build" an onion-domed building by sponge painting with geometric shapes and printing the onion domes on top. After the paint is dry, students can outline or decorate their buildings with markers or crayons.

Bibliography

Aardema, Verna. *Who's in Rabbit's House*. New York, NY: Dial Books, 1977.

Allen, Judy; Earldene McNeill; and Velma Schmidt. *Cultural Awareness for Children*. Reading, MA: Addison-Wesley, 1992.

American Indian Institute. *Oklahoma Indian American School Guide*. Norman, OK: University of Oklahoma Continuing Education, 1979.

Baldwin, Gordon C. *The Apache Indians: Raiders of the Southwest*. New York, NY: Four Winds Press, 1978.

Behrens, June. *Hanukkah: Festivals and Holidays*. Chicago, IL: Childrens Press, 1983.

Bierhorst, John. *Doctor Coyote*. New York, NY: Macmillian, 1987.

Browne, Rollo. *An Aboriginal Family*. Minneapolis, MN: Lerner Publications, 1985.

Cheney, Theodore A. Rees. *Living in Polar Regions*. New York, NY: Franklin Watts, 1987.

Cooper Madlener, Judith. *The Sea Vegetable Gelatin Cookbook*. Santa Barbara, CA: Woodbridge Press, 1981.

Crawshaw, Peter. *Australia*. Englewood Cliffs, NJ: Silver Burdett Press, 1988.

Davis, James E. and Sharryl Davis Hawke. *Tokyo*. Milwaukee, WI: Raintree Publishers, 1990.

Diamond, Judith. *Laos*. Chicago, IL: Childrens Press, 1989.

Dorros, Arthur. *Rain Forest Secrets*. New York, NY: Scholastic, 1990.

Erdoes, Richard. *The Sun Dance People: The Plains Indians, Their Past and Present*. New York, NY: Alfred A. Knopf, 1972.

Ets, Marie Hall. *Nine Days to Christmas*. New York, NY: Viking Press, 1959.

Evans, Patricia. *Rimbles: A Book of Children's Classic Games, Rhymes, Songs, and Sayings*. Garden City, NY: Doubleday, 1961.

Fiarotta, Phyllis and Noel. *Confetti: The Kids' Make-It-Yourself Party Book*. New York, NY: Workman Publishing, 1978.

Germaine, Elizabeth and Ann L. Burckhardt. *Cooking the Australian Way*. Minneapolis, MN: Lerner Publications, 1990.

Gibrill, Martin. *African Food and Drink*. New York, NY: Bookwright Press, 1989.

Israel, Fred L. *Meet the Amish*. New York, NY: Chelsea House, 1986.

Jacobsen, Karen. *South Africa*. Chicago, IL: Childrens Press, 1989.

Johnson, Neil. *Step into China*. New York, NY: Messner, 1988.

Kalman, Bobbie. *Japan—the Culture*. New York, NY: Crabtree Publishing, 1989.

Kalman, Bobbie. *Japan—the People*. New York, NY: Crabtree Publishing, 1989.

Kanitkar, V.P. *Indian Food and Drink*. New York, NY: Bookwright Press, 1987.

Kent, Deborah. *Puerto Rico*. Chicago, IL: Childrens Press, 1992.

Lankford, Mary D. *Hopscotch Around the World*. New York, NY: Morrow Junior Books, 1992.

Lee, Jeanne M. *Toad Is the Uncle of Heaven*. New York, NY: Rinehart and Winston, 1985.

Linse, Barbara. *Art of the Folk*, Larkspur, CA: Art's Publications, 1991.

Lohf, Sabine. *Building Your Own Toys*. Chicago, IL: Childrens Press, 1989.

Minor, Marz and Nono. *The American Indian Craft Book*. Lincoln, NB: University of Nebraska Press, 1972.

Mooney, James. *Cherokee Animal Tales*. New York, NY: Holiday House, 1968.

Morris, Ann. *Hats Hats Hats*. New York, NY: Lothrop, Lee & Shepard, 1989.

National Geographic Society. *The World of the American Indian*. Washington, D.C: National Geographic Society, 1989.

Naylor, Maria. *Authentic Indian Designs*. New York, NY: Dover Publications, Inc., 1975.

Rutledge, Paul. *The Vietnamese in America*. Minneapolis, MN: Lerner Publications, 1987.

Ryden, Hope. *Wild Animals of Africa ABC*. New York, NY: E. P. Dutton, 1989.

Selsam, Millicent E. *Cotton*, New York, NY: William Morrow, 1982.

Shachtman, Tom. *Growing Up Masai*. New York, NY: Macmillan Publishing Co., 1981.

Shalant, Phyllis. *Look What We've Brought You from Vietnam*. New York, NY: Messner, 1988.

Sherlock, Sir Philip. *The Iguana's Tail*. New York, NY: Thomas Y. Crowell, 1969.

Spencer, Robert F. and Jesse D. Jennings. *The Native Americans: Ethnology & Backgrounds of the North American Indians*. New York, NY: HarperCollins, 1977.

Stanek, Muriel. *We Came from Vietnam*. Niles, IL: Albert Whitman & Co., 1985.

Stangl, Jean. *Hats, Hats, and More Hats*. Carthage, IL: Fearon Teacher Aids, 1989.

Stock, Catherine. *Emma's Dragon Hunt.* New York, NY: Lothrop, Lee, & Shepard, 1984.

Tigwell, Tony. *A Family in India.* Minneapolis, MN: Lerner Publications, 1985.

Turner, Dorothy. *Bread.* Minneapolis, MN: Carolrhoda Books, 1989.

Waldman, Carl. *Encyclopedia of Native American Tribes.* New York, NY: Facts on File Publications, 1988.

Watson. R.L. *South Africa in Pictures.* Minneapolis, MN: Lerner Publications, 1988.

Wolfson, Evelyn. *From Abenaki to Zuni: A Dictionary of Native American Tribes.* New York, NY: Walker and Company, 1988.

Wright, David K. *Vietnam.* Chicago, IL: Childrens Press, 1989.

Yue, Charlotte and David. *The Pueblo.* Boston, MA: Houghton Mifflin, 1986.